The Boy and the Old Dam

Dean Schwarz

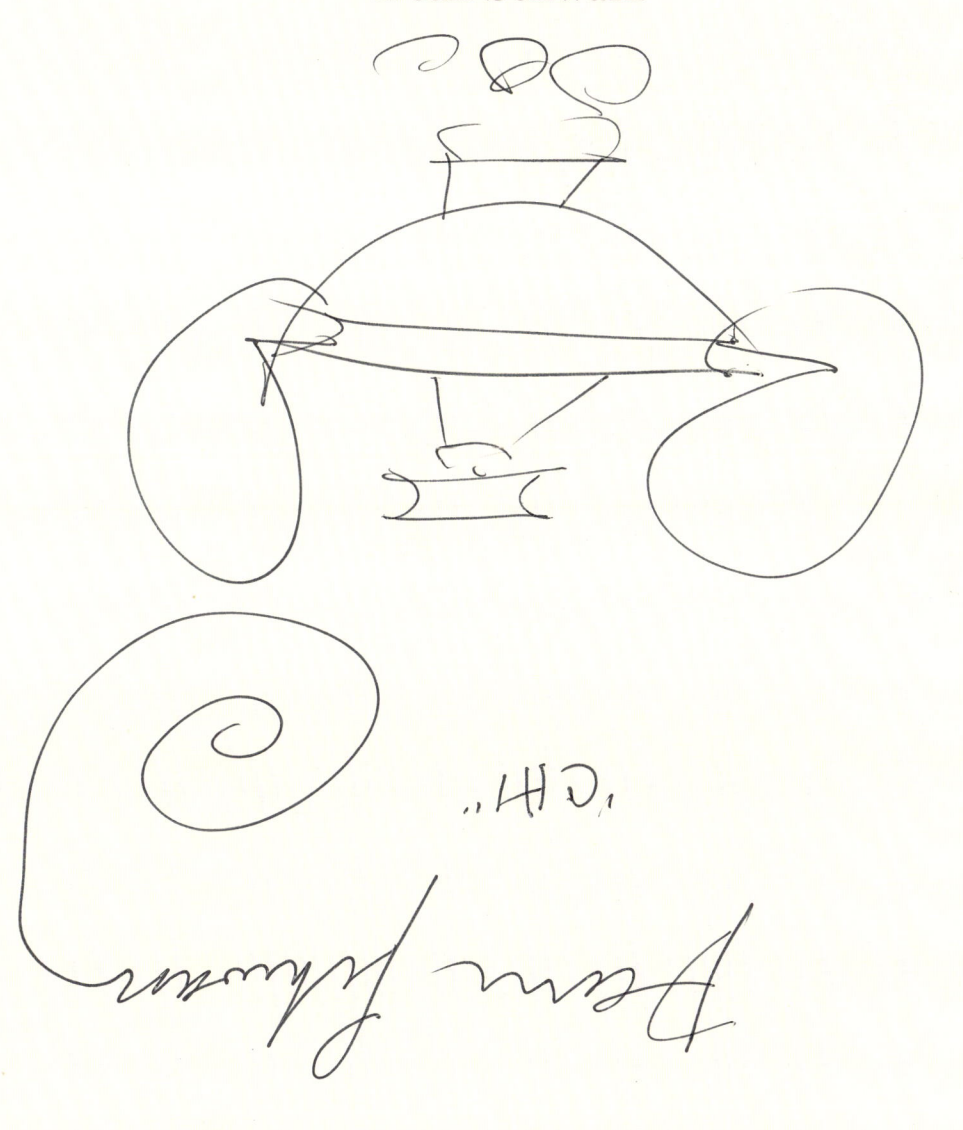

The Boy and the Old Dam

Dean Schwarz

First Edition
© 2014 Dean Schwarz
ISBN: 978-0-615-93678-9
Library of Congress: 2013922471

Published by South Bear Press
2248 South Bear Road
Decorah Iowa 52101
www.southbearpress.org

Geraldine Schwarz, Editor
Jerry Grier, Book Design
Jason Schwarz, Editorial Associate
Dr. John Whelan, Advisor

Printed in Korea through Four Colour Imports, Louisville, KY

Table of Concepts

The Moment
The River
The Old Calcutta
The Routine
The Old Dam Speaks
The Carp
The Danger
The Plank
The 38 Pounder
The Boatlocks
The Victory
The Race
The Zinkers
The Act of Hooky
The Hoard
The Moose
The Pigeons
The E-Gyp-See
The Car-nivore
The Mounds
The Symphony
The Bears
The Sandman
The Coliseum
The Bridge
The Squabs
The Louses
The Games
And Then

THE MOMENT

On a magnificent spring day in the Cedar Rapids that had almost forgotten winter, the Boy and his mother went to the Old Dam for the birth of his memory.

The Boy's mother walked to the dam site pushing the Boy in a stroller. The Boy must have seen the two uncles who sat on the edge of the curving left bank, their bodies drooping to the concrete beyond the hand-smoothed steel safety cables. They were fishing for mudcat but snagging carp. Those round uncles sagged right into their gravitational kinship with the Old Dam. The Boy could not have seen their dangling uncle-legs waving at the water or the return of river's repetitious salutes.

Mother and child were approaching—drawing nearer to the Boy's first memory. He was still a part of his mother. Perhaps, he always would be. A promise of some kind began to emerge. In the four-wheeled stroller, he was no more than its front bumper. He was a large mouth on a skinny frame with two legs projecting forward; yes, he was his mother's bumper.

With the stroller, and the boy's paddle-bottomed shoes, his mother teasingly bumped Uncle Charlie and then Uncle Will toward the drop-off and the hostile water. The muscles and skin of the Boy's face flattened around the place where his nose would eventually grow. He turned white with fear. He felt an immediate enlargement of himself. An unwanted awareness assaulted him. Sounds, smells, brightness, even tastes in the Boy's mouth began.

An awareness of what was to become… began.

Later, he wished he could remember what came before that startling moment. But he couldn't!

So the passing of life and time filled the Boy and the Old Dam with one another.

The Boy's memory grew. Gradually he gained access to language. His motor control developed. His freedoms expanded. Through monthly explanations, weekly corrections, and daily cyclical reminders, his personality was slowly nurtured.

The Boy was lucky, lucky to have a mother and father and an uncle and grandfather and grandmother and to live in such a beautiful spot with the river and the dam.

To him, the Old Dam created the weather they shared. It also established boundary lines—those to be accepted, those to be violated. The Boy knew him or her as a signature of the sacred. Most of the times it was best to stay above his water. But the underside was also good. Maybe best of all was creating questions and violating certain answers. Not knowing something kept learning satisfactory. Even knowing as much as he could, the Boy could not have defined these things. He was better at ask, ask, asking… questions, questions. And he was great at selectively forgetting any that he chose not to remember.

The Old Dam was an ever-changing gateway from where life flowed, where no two seconds of creation were the same, where every image is beautiful. A place where being grateful is easy.

The image of the Old Dam was in the Boy, that is true, but the structure of the Old Dam was smaller than the inherent image. Would the Old Dam suggest such thoughts? Prolly-not. The Old Dam was… just was, and how!

He always called it the Old Dam, knowing that it was much more than just concrete and steel.

THE RIVER

Water was the Dam's best buddy. Water was what finally made the proportions perfect. More especially on a day when summer puff-clouds were climbing out of the Water into the Dam and up, ever up, up into, and even out of the top of the sky.

If the Dam and the Water had a mother, she would have discouraged their friendship. They took turns getting each other into trouble. But, nary a day did they part. Never. The changing seasons changed the buddies' character every day. But, what was the flat out character of the Old Dam? That question caused the Boy's leaning into learning the nature and the Nature of The Middle Aged River at The Old Dam (School).

When that school was closed for winter vacation, the Old Dam and the River took hibernation recesses. The slack-brown Water above the Dam turned itself into a surprisingly thick white quilt, ironed so smooth that there wasn't even a dinky wave. Or even a ripple to be seen. Each of its many feet, and each-and-every watery toe of the River was completely tucked in under the yearly brand-new quilt. The Boy had watched his Aunt Toots make quilts but this was so fast, so complete, and with such small stitches that the Boy couldn't even see them.

In great contrast to the opaque quilt cover, the open Water between the Dam and the F Avenue Bridge was a marvelously black mirror. Or so the Boy thought, and thought again. By walking to an exact spot on the F Avenue Bridge, when the sun was in a specific position, the Boy could finger-step while counting down on shelf after shelf into the Water's very self, its introspective self.

If the River's quilt was a glacier, its work was only beginning, becoming. In the next few days it grew thicker, ever thicker. And if the quilt had a tongue, it was sticking it out in an upstream direction while growing longer and freezing, even longer saying, "Boom, boom, b-boom," while cracking, "Boom, boom, ba-boomba."

The Boy paid much more attention to the igloo's drum when he was walking on its ice (which was not recommended). Those booms were the reports of mile long fractures in thick ice crack-bam-b-booming. The sounds were as beautiful as the coyotee calls from across the River in the depths of the railroad yards between the River and Cedar Lake, which all the coyotees knew, really knew, as the Slough, the Slooo—, … It was so mournful when the coyotees said Sl-ooooo. It was a drawn out affair—first one would hear a ba-boomba, or a Who who, who-who? Who who, who-who? Who who who-awk! of a Quaker Oat owl, each and every eeder or eyeder sound in the early night would invite a concert by the coyotes and/or the Oat owls, and of course the ba-boomb-ahs initiated stanza after stanza. Those things happened on those winter days when the Boy's teacher reported to the Boy's mother that the Boy didn't listen.

By late winter the igloo became a turtle shell. Then Thirty-Three Degrees came to town with the equinox. The fourth time they did that they broke the turtle's back. The shards raged downstream as a jig-saw-puzzle which one might put back together as a farm field of rich black soil, which was now brown, very brown water, filled with fragments of farm houses, sheds and barns leaping over the dam and repetitiously lurching up to scour the under-bellies of the F Avenue, 1st Avenue, 2nd Avenue and 3rd Avenue bridges. The Boy wanted to be everywhere all at once. During these River rages the bridges were bleachers filled with fans, losing fans. One said, "There sure are a-la-da-sad farms in town."

After the spectacle was over because half of the Water had gone down stream, the Old Dam rested. During the Time-to-Reconnoiter, the Boy's mother shifted her attention to wild flowers and mush-roons. The Boy turned from subtraction to addition. Soon Mother Nature turned life into multiplication. Then during the long-getting-longer-days, before the nippy short days showed up again, he counted and recounted how the dam divided the river into nine equal parts and one unequal boatlocks and one broken-down fish ladder. He watched the dam cull a perfect amount of the river and direct it into the millrace, on the side of the dam he knew the least about, near where his grand father had built the fourth pioneer log house in Cedar Rapids on the Cedar rapids where the Old Dam now lived.

Of course, the Boy did eventually learn much more about most of these things and many more about the Old Dam and what it taught, and what it might still teach. After all, the life of this boy, and this dam, became one life as seasons flowed downstream through the living room of the Boy: his River and his Dam.

Did the Boy ever learn the answer to his father Frank's old question, "What will it be like when all the River water runs downstream?"

THE OLD CALCUTTA

In the Boy's eighth March through the months, the melt sent spectacular slabs of ice over the Old Dam right on time. If all proceeded according to the Boy's wishes, even the icy "fingers of April dawn" along the catwalk would melt. The days lengthened, and when night slowly came, the lights on the F Avenue Bridge turned warmer, and much friendlier than they had been since October.

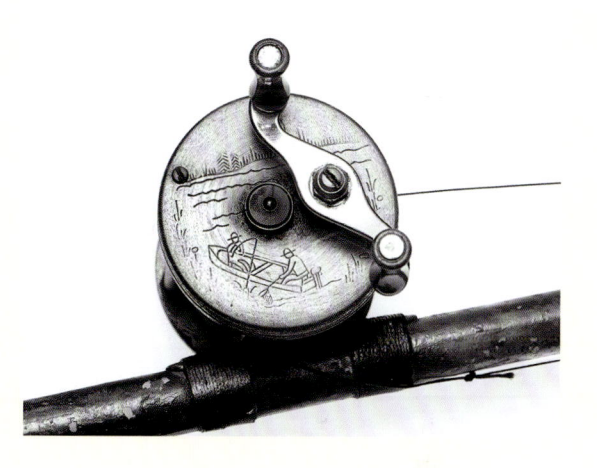

By May the Boy's uncles were usually at their posts. Those posts were the best spots where catfish and crappies bit. Uncle Charlie thought river, thought fish. Charlie could read the river's currents. He could translate the calligraphic splashes of frightened minnows. He knew who autographed certain swirls in the water.

Father-Uncle Charlie used a Calcutta-cane pole with a Silver Neptune reel. One outside of the reel had a picture of a young buckskinned woman, kneeling on her knees, presenting a fish. The other side was etched with the image of the ancient Greek God Neptune who looked like the Boy's Uncle Charlie, but without glasses and with a beard. Behind Neptune, pine trees stood within a perfect circle. The circle represented a full moon or perhaps the sun, the Boy thought. "It was rilly beauty-full." (He wasn't-at-all-sure about that girl.)

Charlie had made the pole. He had carefully wrapped the eyes, the tip, and seated the reel with black nylon twenty-pound test line, the same beautifully braided stream of line he used to catch fish.

His hand remembered the skills the ancestors used to make the wrappings while each finger recalled its evolution of movement, its finger-to-hand-to-mouth duties. The Old-Ones knew that the tools the hand made required more than their best craftsmanship. Life and death were involved. Within such craft there is a large something that goes beyond the hand. Heart? Spirit? Charlie had paid great attention to the eyes of the Old Calcutta. From the tips of his fingers came knots from ancients, archaics, aborigines and boatswain mates. The Old Calcutta was lastly covered with layers on layers of shellac to preserve a tactile tradition that even Homer would be proud of. The Old Calcutta became a portrait of a human as a fishing pole. In years to come, such gifts would become even more and more important to future generations.

The pole's vision became greater than its maker's. Is it a fact that an eagle's eye is about the size of a human eye? The Old Calcutta's eyes were much smaller, but just the same, they were larger. This is the stuff of life that the Boy was learning.

By total emersion in fish, the pole was inaugurated as the Old Calcutta. Its many battles with fish and mysterious snags helped it grow into a large permanent curve, almost a C. It looked like an archer's bow even when its line was not stretched from eye to reel. It stayed bent as if it was continually fighting fish. Or, perhaps it was imploring to be taken fishing when it stood at home in the corner, ossifying.

Other than Charlie, no one had such a pole. Yet they all had ideas about how the bend got there. But, no one asked Charlie, more than once.

Charlie hated budging budgers. He'd tell them to butt out when they squirmed, like a fish worm, into his spot after he'd caught a fish. But he was generous, always generous, with the Boy. "There's one bite-n right down there," he'd say, "See-if-ya–can-get-it. Maybe you can snag Old Man What's-his-name's false teeth—he lost 'em in there last week and he hadn't even paid for 'em yet."

But then, the Boy would hardly ever catch a fish. He was too impatient. His line would be in the water, a minute here, a moment there. Usually, he would just be there. He'd be there for every minute he could. The Boy acted out a wide interpretation of the word fishing. Father-Uncle Charlie was a magician, and at the Dam he preformed his magic. The Boy didn't want to miss any of it.

THE ROUTINE

Usually it was on weekends. The Boy's father and the uncles would let him come along. Sometimes.

They pulled into a gravel driveway by the F Avenue Bridge and parked behind the Farmers' Market. The Boy was making little anxiously excited movements full of observations. There was just time enough for a quick smile as he bailed out of the car realizing that the car was parked, just so, so it too could watch the fun that was about to begin.

Each of the men pulled his hip boots up from knee to crotch and hooked the rubber straps over his belt. The Boy could smell excitement swelling up from the boots and the men.

The Boy wanted boots, too, but his All Star sneakers were sweller.

The men were preparing to seine craw-crawdad-crawdaddies and mini-minoso-minnows.

The men side-stepped down the steep limestone step-bank to the River. The Boy gollied the River, and lurched into the watery little song he whistled each time he greeted it. "Settle down," groused Uncle Will amid the mallard quacks rising from their green, golden-glowing heads that begged for bread crumb-chunks.

The Boy tried to make his lips into the shape of the curved bills of the quackers. But he couldn't overcome the smile of his lip-curves. What he also heard, but didn't pay much attention to, was a background grousing of men, mixed with foreground protestations of the ducks as they swam away, maybe hungry.

It sure was a curious contrast to see how easily the body-boat-ducks glided above the frantic churning of their paddlewheel feet.

The uncles and the dad didn't seem to notice. But how would the Boy know that? He was wading upstream, backwards, quacking in a multiplication table of watery adventures ending and beginning. So the Boy fell into the water. So what? He got up so fast that he didn't get wet.

Just when did the Boy start thinking of the crawdad pinchers? He wasn't old enough to have lived a long history of any subject. But, in his imagination, pinchers can grow quickly into the "hu-mong-ous..." (The Boy would have liked to have thought that he invented this word out of an idea of a verb flashing spinner-bait, a barbed hook of grammar and lead sinkers of multiple misspellings. But he didn't have the slightest idea what a verb was. But he was very good at the lead sinkers.)

The magnetism of the men's actions near a Crawdad Castle attracted him and directed him through eddies of flashing River waterzizim and boyzizm, only to be pinched anyway by a giant (the one-claw kings are the biggest and the worstest) pain daddies. But…

Not so fast—

Craw-da dee-daddies, and no-crawl claw grand craw daddies, crawdiddadies-boots, Crawl d-d-dad-ee nets, seines. Do crawdaddies always crawldaddies backwards? Shooting star crawdaddies do.

Dad.

Claw-da dee-daddies, and no-claw grand daddies, clawdiddad-boots, Claw yes in-deed, daddies, crawldads, clawdads, and pincher pincer clawdaddies. Ouch!

Do Dad do (pull off the pinzers) do.

Under the bridge there was a chute of fast water over a rocky bottom. Uncle Charlie and Uncle Will held the broken broom handles fastened to the ends of the fifteen-foot seine. When they dipped the seine into the Water, the current carried the center of it downstream causing it to form a mighty curve, Old Calcutta like. The Boy saw a white froth of water rush through the square holes in the seine while he was looking for the spacing of the lead sinkers that were searching for the bottom. If the uncles didn't keep the handles and the sinkers on the riverbed, the crawdaddies shot under the seine, under the rocks, into their front doors. But, everything was perfect—even the corks that liked the top of the water were behaving.

Now it was Frank's turn. He stepped off the dry rocks onto the wet ones, the deeper and a-little deeper ones, thrashing the water and splashing like a crazy kid, a great big kid that didn't use any water deeper than his boots.

Should an ignorant passerby on the bridge see this, he might consider… insanity? The crawdads certainly did. They saw two monsters coming downstream together, kicking in the roofses of their houseses. Were the monsters trees, the did-daddies must have wondered, looking for a place to root? Above the roof kickers a dark shadow or a foreboding cloud could be seen between the water and the arch of the F Avenue Bridge. The dark cloud and the terrible rootless tree was Frank, the crawdad herder.

This excitement was nothing, though, when trying not to think of pinchers. Pinchers! Yet the Boy didn't want to show this weakness to his family.

In his big boots, the Boy's father waded and waddled and danced upstream of the net, churning and turning the stones on the riverbed. He sent the crawdads backwards, downstream, shooting like stars in every direction, mostly toward the seine.

Minnies were accepted by the minnow bucket, but not sought after because the mission of this specific expedition was trot lining. And with trot lining, "Crawdads stay on the hook better," the Boy was taught-told.

With a full minnow pail, all crawdad pinchers were removed. (What about the hard-shell-daddy that only had one pincher, the craw-claw, king-daddy the Boy had seen?) Its remaining pincher made up for two regular pinchers. The Boy thought he saw two eyes on that scary pincher. "What about that giant pincher guy, did you break his wanna-be pincher off before you put it in the pail," the Boy asked?

Uncle Will reached into the pail, saying, "Do you mean this one?" In an instant, his hand came out of the pail and tossed a fake clawdaddydaddy at the Boy. Through the laughter of the men, the Boy splashed over backwards again. But his recovery was so fast that even though he got doused good, he didn't get wet. He didn't want the men to know that the trick had gotsted him good.

Without a word the fishermen climbed the bank and got into the Model T. Uncle Will drove up to the CNW railroad bridge, singing, "the Chicago and North Western line…"

They walked down to where the boat was tied. Everyone knew his job. Frank manned the oars, maneuvered the boat. His job was to keep the bow of the boat facing directly into the current while the crew carried on their activities.

Uncle Will reached over the side of the boat and down into the water through a wavy sun and the nervous image of Quaker Oats. He tied the end of the heavy trot line to the root of a bank willow. His sure knot was carefully tied, just below the water, where he hoped it would not be discovered by a poacher.

Uncle Charlie removed the oh-so organized smaller lines, the weights and the hooks from his tackle box. They then played-out the main line as Father Frank slowly rowed toward the other bank. Uncle Will used double hitches to tie the smaller lines, and tied their large hooks onto the main line. Charlie did the baiting. Single crawdads were impaled from the tip of the tail right through their translucent meat. The hook continued up and was driven out at the toughest point, which was between the ever-crawling crawdad legs. The Boy helped by hooking three minnies to every fourth hook.

It was very difficult to keep the boat moving into deeper and deeper water while the line played out and over the middle of the boat during the preparations. On rare occasions, a hook would nip the workers, or a defeugalty would scrape the skin of the crew's impatience. These were events worthy of oral ejaculations. The Boy loved this cussing. It was easy to learn the how and the when of it, because of the tone and pompous circumstances of its pronunciation. However, he was not permitted to participate. His opportunities were saved and practiced in his mind, in this case his very active mind, for his buddies, later. From his seat the Boy practiced numerous expectations.

As the uncles peeled the line, he could see the baits dangling down. Downstream, the safety cable above the dam looked like the large shadow of the trotline.

Since he sometimes ate boiled crawdads, he knew the fish would like them. More especially the big soft-shelled crawl-daddies.

When all the hooks were ready, the line was stretched, and the large stone tied to its end was released to find the river bottom. All that remained now was luck, the Boy thought.

Four hours later they returned to run the line. They had hooked two carp and a large blue catfish. "That cool blue is as beautiful as a strawberry popsicle on a sizzling day," said the Boy to himself.

The Boy's mother cooked the catfish and the Boy helped finish it off. His dad didn't eat no fish. The Boy's mother cooked a hamburger for him.

One of the carp, the Boy sold for twenty-five cents to a Jewish neighbor. The Boy thought that was perfect. The fish he liked, he ate. The fish he didn't like, he got a nickel for. His parents got the other twenty cents. Perfect! And the neighbors were happy, too. They couldn't eat fish without scales? The other carp, the Boy's father smoked. The Boy thought, "The Old Dam and the Water like all of their fish."

THE OLD DAM SPEAKS

At flood stage the Old Dam looked young. His piers looked strong, very strong. They were smoothly parallel and ready to meet any crisis. Generations of floods never saw the old in the Old Dam. To the floods the Dam's muscles were determined bones of contention. They never knew the all-year-around Dam that the Boy knew. Floods never saw the sleepy summer-endin' Dam or the fall times that brought the Boy's last swim of the year. Fall found the Dam yawnin' in-a swimsuit, wearing old sneakers in the water below his ancient ankles.

The Boy never questioned how the Old Dam could have so many personalities.... Each rhythmic year the Old Dam played hide and seek with his ankles. The Boy marveled at the space where concrete used to be—at the roughness and barked sharpness of the rocks that were obviously harder than the concrete that used to cover them. Yet the Boy could not have put it just like that. He only sensed that the Old Dam was prolly just like this when the uncles—and his father, and his father's father—had been boys there. Yet, he knew that the old ankles had once been young.

He knew there had been a time when the reinforcement rods hid in The Old Dam's concrete as invisible blood vessels, not like the way they were now as on the steel-working arms of his grampa. The Boy never seemed to know enough about the Old Dam. Was it a teacher, coach, pastor…? Certainly not just these!

And how did the calendar and the clock interfere with his Old-Dam-time? How did the weather? How did the seasons? How did...? Why?

In swirlpools of questions and the slack waters of answers, the Boy studied his Dam. It could be guessed that the Old Dam studied its Boy, too.

The changes in the levels of the water always fascinated the Boy. Those spaces exposed between the highest and lowest points of the river's annual personality were an encyclopedia. The Old Dam read its story out loud to him in a way that could be understood in a progression of detection and accumulation, just as archaeologists read old potsherds to curious current cultures. The Boy loved to be read to. He never wanted the good book to end.

In the case of high water, the Boy could see, or at least imagine, the highest level the water had reached. Because, after all, only two blocks away on the Russell's Velvet Ice Cream building under "It's Pure That's Sure," there was a line painted and a year given. The date was back when time was measured before the Boy (1929).

He imagined other things measured in ice cream times, too. Yes he did. He thought thoughtly thoughts like, wasn't there a River before that building and the line on the building? He was learnin' to think River: An expanding raging River is a no-good-fishing River, and a retreating River is a getting-ready to be a rilly-good-fishin' River!

He wondered where that Russell's Velvet Ice Cream flood-line had been drawn on his house, and on his school and, with a smile, on his father's hip boots. Was the line… a map, or the Water's signature? It was the edge of a trail. The Boy was caught worrying where it might be drawn next.

So a cement Dam and a powerful River became and became in the Boy.

When he later thought back on his life with the Dam, there were many visual and tactile experiences that he associated with its seasons and the changes between them.

His favey-favorite months were the thunder-boomer months of popping popcorn clouds, mmm, summertime. Knowing, but pushing back by ("Improving on the truth,") the Boy lived away-away the coming flat

13

pancake clouds of autumn skies that would become worser 'n worser universes of winter, winter gray gray gray-flat clouds that could only be sweetened by spring's maple syrup-cooking, mmm,,,,, "Oh sweet springtime, Keep springtime and summer just for me," said the Boy.

Welcome home, thunder-boomers.

THE CARP

Then, once upon a summer swelter, there was a whiff, a sniff of stink stinkers. The smell of another very explicit time began. It wafted from low, lowdown sources to the heights of the western riverbank where it was not sooo strong. Nor was it so strong from the boatlocks, or from first-pier. The Boy could certainly tell you that. It rose from the mud-cracked rocks on the Dam's canyon floor, where first a peninsula and then an island had emerged when summer's water almost disappeared (downstream). From there anyone, and everyone, could smell it. But almost no one came there. No one wanted to visit this Boy's living room.

The Boy could clearly remember when he first examined one of the dead carp lying there. Most of them were five or six pounders. "Let's see," the Boy added, (he was good at adding when it was quarters or dimes and nickels), "that's prolly three dollars and a nickel's worth." The carp's large scales had bloated away from one another. Different from live ones, he thought. These were edged and slightly washed with mud. He was reminded of the doilies on the padded arms of the couch in his gramma's living room. Those arms were about the same size as the dead fish. About five or six pounders.

Gramma Schwarz's living room was not a living room. It was a room in which the Boy was expected to hold his breath while he passed through it on his way to the front porch. He had to hold his breath often because he liked to glide with his quite grand grand mother and his moderately grand (in size) grand father on their green steel glider that glided on the porch outside of the living room.

Sitting together the three made a comfortable san-wich of conversation. The old grands were crusty slices of German bread. The Boy was the skimpy-skinny Spam squeezed between them.

Gramma was describing a spattering she received from a shite-poke, which she often called a shit-pike. He learned that these terms referred to a bird that was a not-so-little little green heron or to another of her favorites, the very-great, great blue heron. His gramma seemed to know a great deal about the history of their activities near the Old Dam. Apparently these birds were local, well-known, aerial bombers and/or critics famous for their physically directed criticisms toward fishermen and their cars. Gramma recited these crits with great humor. She often warned the Boy to watch out for the shite-pokes.

When occasions to sit in the living room did occur, subjects like those feathered critics never touched the lips of the Boy's then extremely-grand-mother. At those times humor seemed to have been left out on the front porch to swing on the glider, alone. The Boy rested one arm on the carp doily, in silence. He leaned back into the big doily minnow net that his grandmother had crocheted.

After escaping from that net, his thoughts returned. How he had escaped from the putrid stink, he wanted to know, because he desperately desired to escape again. His curiosity did help him though. The Boy eyed the Dam's dead carp. They seemed to be looking for their missing eyeballs.

Some of the blimps, the carcass humps, the vacant fish on limestone plates—some of those muddy capped carp were moving. How can? He wondered the why of it.

He turned one with a stick.

"Jeepers!"

His nose jerked back, his eyes followed, flooding. The carp was alive in a putrid pudding of boiling rice. The Boy's eyes, commanded by his nose, rebelled. His stomach began to speak in convolutions of almost eruptions. The Boy was learning his first lesson in maggotology. Later, he learned to be bothered by them and later still, not to be. Death and life continued to dance in a fascinating rhythm.

Wherever he saw old dams on rides with his parents—like the Upper and Lower dams, the dam at Mitchell, and the one by a restaurant in Iowa City—yes, wherever he saw old dams, he saw dancing carp. And again yes, he would smell the rhythm of blind carp dancing.

It wasn't bad, it just was.

Then, to divert his own attention, "Suckers and goldfish," the Boy whispered, "and buffalo and armadillo." He liked to play with River words. It was not just nonsense-fun. He enjoyed arranging and rearranging words.

Yes,

suckers and goldfish, buffalo and sheephead and armadillo grew in his nomenclature of carp. Carpsuckers, reticulated and unreticulated carpsuckers, quillback, redhorse, sheephead, shiners, suckers and goldfish and buffalo and armadillo.

He went on and on, thinking in his own private dimension.

It was his Father-Uncle Charlie who taught him that goldfish were carp. His Uncle Rodman taught him reticulated and unreticulated. ...gold and buffalo fish and armadillo and kakemonos. He, himself, coined armadillo, for his dead carp, and kakemono was his Uncle-Father Clayton's. "Clayton was a doctor somethin'," a fisherman of a kind, but more a type of a hunter, a fowler. He taught the Boy that kakemonos were Japanese scrolls where carp forever swam as symbols for hardiness in boys.

The hardiness part, and the rhythm of the word kakemono, pleased the Boy because they fit his musings and the rhythms of his Old Dam. Also, because his Father-Uncle Clayton had taken his chew-stubbed cigar to another world, one where he could "fish" from the back of a live camel.

The Boy missed his Uncle-Dr.-Clayton. He missed him, even though the Boy didn't completely enjoy the fact that his uncle called him, "Dumb Guy." With that expression his uncle had never failed to get the Boy's attention.

The whip of that term was a painfully good teacher. "Dumb Guy" was never used when it was inappropriate. "Dumb Guy" was not related to correctional usage of words by the Sloppy Swearing family. "Dumb Guy" caused the Boy to reflect on and to correct his mistakes.

The Boy returned to his *elegy*.

Suckers: and goldfish, and buffalo and armadillo. Suckers in gold fish holes, buffalo and sheephead, armadillos. Carpsucker, reticulated and unreticulated quillback carpsuckers: redhorse; sheephead; shiners. Suckers and goldfish-fish, fish for buffalo and armadillo: kakemonos.

The Boy didn't like high water. It meant that the river would close. When the river was way up, life sank miserably to things like playing marbles. Besides, the Boy already had all of Leo's marbles. And Leo was the only other boy who lived on Summer Street.

Ronnie Young lived around the corner, but he was always *read*-ing.

Then there was baseball. It was just above homework, when he thought about it. It always improved though, when he was playing. Nothing could compare to the Old Dam. When the river was up, it was drats! Drats, drats!

There was just no participating with high water, with angry water. It really was true, the life of the river did close. So the Boy asked Leo if he had any new marbles, but he didn't.

So, the Boy went to bed, forced to be content with sleeping in crawdad-and-minnow-pool dreams. Content with the nightmarish repeating of the sound of Miss Diemon's baseball-picture window breaking—a sound he had heard earlier when he was not sleeping.

Even from his dreams the Boy could hear the dam's exclamation. Closed! Closed!

In the morning the Boy headed for the Old Dam to see if the river was open yet, even though he could hear that it wasn't.

The Boy crossed Summer Street at a rakish northeast angle, passed Leo's house that didn't look like a house at all. It looked just like a gray-green wall. Then he rounded the corner and looked carefully up and down F Avenue before making a dash for it. On the far curb he walked toward the bridge, then turned left beyond the mouth of Hawkeye Lumber into the graveled triangle formed by the huge sign, "Best Lumber Yard By a Dam Site," and the concrete curve of the high bank of the river's western edge where his uncles often sat.

The Boy passed the boat locks, already very disappointed because the river was even higher. He walked about a half block upstream, on the dark overgrown path on top of the dike. The path reached up four blocks toward Hubbard Ice and its mountainous sand piles, eventually up to a curve where the road met Ellis Avenue. But his immediate destination was only as far as the footings that supported a rusty safety cable that reached across the river above the dam. Once there, the Boy sat in the little clearing, his toes just above the water. The big cable reached over to a similar footing on the far bank near Quaker Oats. It looked like a tired telephone wire with lines dangling at intervals of about every fifty feet.

He didn't want to be sure, (a word that the Boy and his distant country friend, Jimmy Milota, pronounced as "chew-er." The Boy's mother thought that was cute.) He didn't want to be sure that he had witnessed the tragedy that happened there, that day, but he was sure never-the-less. And he was sure that he had been told about it. A million and one times.

"Be careful," his mother always said.

And his father added, "You listen to your mother, now."

THE DANGER

The boat was out of control!

This fact pierced the Boy, as it approached the safety cable, as it neared a dangling steel rope that was far out from the one that twisted down above the Boy.

Pain sprang out of the Boy's chest. Fear speared him repeatedly. It must have already attacked the boat's men and its child.

With an oar, one man paddled crazily left, toward the steel rope hanging closest to the boat. Nearing it, both men became tiny, with large hands, stretching far out. One man, in the bow, grasped the rusty strands. His grip on the cable caused the boat to spin quickly around in the current, end to end, throwing the other man to the deck, the oar into the river.

The Boy, who could not see the child, had reached up, like a mimic, at the same time as the men had, catching hold of the hanging shore-side cable.

When the boat spun, it jerked the cable from the Boy's hand, sending rusty steel slivers into his fingers as it sling-shot free, into the air.

In the instant when the boat and the Boy were on their steel ropes, he saw them each as carp hooked on his father's trotline.

The boat looked safe. The Boy relaxed. He released a huge sigh.

Then, in a measuring of time that the Boy had never before witnessed, simply, the boat again filled with panic. The man had lost his grip. The boat was backing down the river, in a slow witless way.

Fear again was at Neptune's spears. The Boy was wounded with pain. Obviously, so were the boaters.

Why? The Boy might have shouted. How? It had looked so secure.

Now the cable was empty, a marker only, measuring, perhaps, the boat's reluctant, backward acceleration. A hopeless resignation descended. The Boy could not remember the men and still did not see the child, as the boat drifted further down from the cable toward the dam. But he did remember a clock-throbbing heartbeat in his hand.

When the boat disappeared into the turbulence over the dam, the Boy's movement began. He must have told himself to run. To speed down to the spot on the F Avenue Bridge, below the dam. He must have. To where a small clot of people were coagulated in horror. Once arriving, the Boy never saw anything other than what he always saw from there in high water.

So he ran downstream, past the outdoor market, down to the First Avenue Bridge. Nothing there either. Down to the Second Avenue bridge for more of the same.

At the Third Avenue Bridge, between the Court House and the CRANDIC Railroad Bridge, two fire trucks and several police cars were arriving.

He heard someone crying. And another. A girl had a handkerchief and a bloody nose. But the Boy saw nothing in the river except turbulence, foam and reflections.

Dumb, helpless, time reeling out, the Boy's strength flowed down his body into his shoes as if he was a thermometer on a day when the temperature plunged.

Hours later, maybe, long after his mother's unheard call for supper, he walked aimlessly back up to and past the dirge of the Old Dam. Back to the little clearing with its cable. One sore hand throbbed in the other as he walked.

He sat down again, and looked upstream toward the erector set that, in earlier light, had been a railroad bridge.

The safety cable still reached out, and still saved nothing except its own footing across the raging river. It looked like a ladder, the bottom side under water, its rungs searching for its better half.

One hand still held the other. He thought, those cables look like anyone could have caught them. He said it again, quietly, but this time out loud, to the Old Dam. "Those cables look like anyone could have caught them.

He watched the fast river, his thoughts racing. Little pieces of foam were skimming downstream like they always did when the water was high. It was not pulled directly like the boat had been, but being whipped, this way and that, by every whim of the wind. The foam was not water, not air. Yet, it was not as free as it looked because it was affected by the general direction of the river's flow. But, the foam was water, was air. How could it be, and not be, the same thing? The Boy thought.

He was propelled by boy-thoughts that moved him just as the foam was moved, by wind-thoughts and river-thoughts. By Old Dam thoughts, too?

The thunder in his sore hand taught the Boy questions. Quick questions. Questions that could stand alone. They were a sponge fuzz, froth caught in the beard of the River. Caught in the frenzy of the Red Cedar.

Only in moments of extreme focus or subconscious stimulation would the Boy glimpse their answers.

Most of the time the Boy did not even know which were the most important, the answers or the questions.

Then the thunderbeat in his hurted hand revealed something. From somewhere straight out of an unfamiliar retrospect, he saw what he hadn't seen before. His vision seemed to focus from above the tower of the cable.

He saw the man, sickened by the loss of his grip on the safety cable, grope in the bottom of the boat and find the remaining oar. The man stood and paddled frantically. The Boy saw this in slow motion, like looking back to a life preserved in fossilized stone. He saw every detail. He could feel how heavy the oar was, unlike a canoe paddle. He knew the color of the oar, could touch the oar's pitted metal collar, its shiny pin. He heard the pin flop and strike the wooden oar every time the man paddled. The Boy smelled the man's fear-laced sweat.

He saw and felt the depth of a feeling that became painfully clear. He realized that it didn't matter how hard the man tried.

Then, when the boat was thirty, or twenty-five, or twenty feet from the dam, he saw the man drop the oar and grab the gunnels of the boat.

Suddenly, the image disappeared.

Sitting there under the rusty cable, the Boy's mind returned to his questions. A whirlpool of questions.

Then, the questions were interrupted by another image. With the speed, the clarity, and the perfect memory of a box camera, he saw the girl.

Just as quickly the throbbing questions returned from his hurted hand. Click, click, click, the questions themselves, asked questions, before they again turned themselves back into images, click. Each image was both complete and developing, somehow creating its own life. His hand and his mind danced.

In another click was the precept of the Old Dam's figure.

Why and what-had-he-seen questions inundated him.

The image of the girl was gone. Only the questions about the girl would remain. He failed when he tried to match the image with the girls he knew. They didn't fit.

Where was the figure of the Old Dam?

From where had the image of the girl come? Where? His hurted hand found no answer.

Dizzily the scene began again, from the start. The boat drifted toward the cable and did all the things it did before.

The whole scene repeated itself again. And again. Out of the thunderstorm in the hand, and??? … the Boy received more questions...

Why did the boat float into his life? How many times would he have to watch it? How did this event, these people, become so suddenly important to him?

Then a question was produced that even the Boy thought was crazy. Did the boat somehow float straight into the dam itself?

These images, ideas and questions, the chiefest among them, the last one, remained with the Boy, in his dullness.

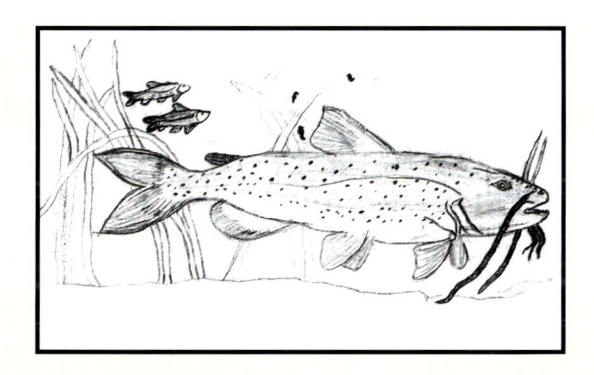

They never found the body of the boat.
The Boy had to get a tetanus shot.
The river slowly opened again.
Then he was told that they finally found the bodies of the men.
And, the little girl?
"She was wearing a doily," a fisherman had said.
"A little, crocheted, mud caked, smock," his wife corrected.

"She's a blind dancer," the Boy said,
but only the Old Dam was listening.

THE PLANK

The Boy was eight. He was scrawny. His uncle Will called him Weenie. He was a feisty weenie, for eight.

No matter how hard the Boy tried, he could not be more than eight (Yet). And despite the fact that he couldn't be, he tried anyway. The Boy always wanted to be something he wasn't. However, he did display a great deal of pride in the fact that he <u>had</u> reached that great number. Eight seemed magic!

There is no doubt about it. The Boy's first real challenge was received at the boatlocks.

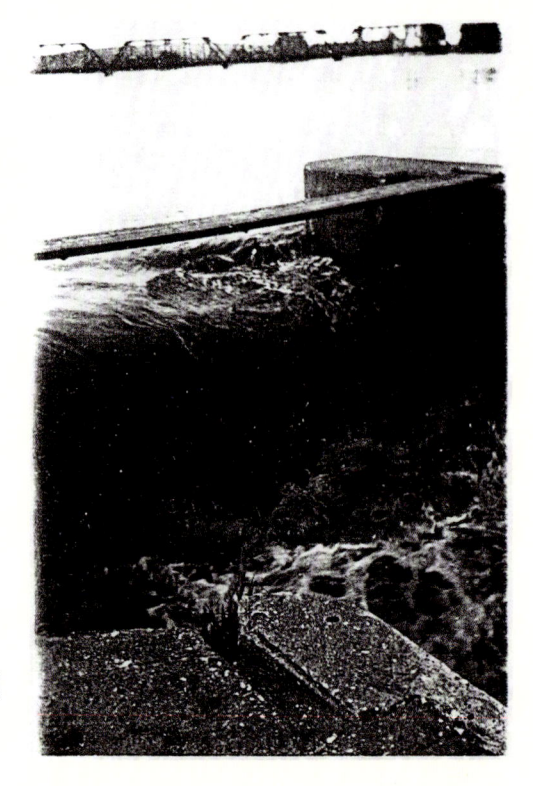

Big men could accomplish it. The Boy watched them do it (often).

So the Boy knew the plank wouldn't break.

Men whose bellies bulged over wide black belts (black belts that were not big enough to surround those bellies) could do it. The belts became so tight; they pulled so hard against the men's backs that the men's butts had nearly disappeared. Yes, they could do it.

One man who wore two pup tents could do it. One tent was for each leg— tents like the one the Boy had found camped under his fifth Christmas tree. In the eyes and on the tongue of someone so teeny, the man was a Hip-o-less Pot-o-mass. Sooo… the Boy knew it wouldn't break.

Then the Boy saw the kid, one he had seen at the CSPS Hall, tumbling and working out on the balance beam.

That kid didn't just do it. He danced it. He danced, the fox; he trotted, across the obstacle. Just who was that fox, that trot?

The kid had haughtily, or arrogantly, or nonchalantly, or spiritually, crossed. The Boy didn't know these words, but he would learn them from just such actions. The Boy knew that the kid certainly didn't cross in fear. Swagger, now there was a good word. Braggadocio. Vainglory. The Boy knew the action; he wanted to become the kid. He would search for the right words later.

As if in contrast, two enormous identical twin fishermen, in step, lumbered across in cadence, right behind the kid. Each wore hip boots. Each carried a full minnow pail, fish poles, a big tackle box and brown sack lunches.

Now the Boy knew for "chew-er" that it wouldn't break. The challenge must be faced!

A formidable board caused all the Boy's hedging. It was made of oak and had no handrail. The board that reached across the upper end of the boatlocks was actually two bridge planks. There was a wide crack between them. A crack the Boy could see through. Clearly. Perhaps the plank was twenty-four or even twenty-six inches wide. But to the Boy it seemed no wider than the balance beam at the CSPS Hall.

The plank afforded fishermen access to the dam from the west bank and stuck out its long tongue at the Boy.

The water above the plank was usually a calm lake, flat and mellow. But still, it was eight feet down. And the water looked deep.

Downstream from the plank, the water was a turbulent river, eighteen feet below. It was actively creating off-white foam.

The waterfall was directly under the plank. The Boy saw it, all too plainly, right through the crack.

The Boy had placed his foot on the western end of the plank many times. But he then got, or thought he got, dizzy, so he withdrew that foot. He was casual though.

His one step forward, pause, one step backward, pause (fish for a while): one step forward, pause, one step backward, pause (fish) rhythm, he had danced, but he had not choreographed. Yes, the Boy danced it many times. It was somewhat like the "brush tap-step, brush tap-step," tap dance lessons he unwillingly danced at the CSPS Hall. He danced in the same room where the gymnasts were dancing a dance he liked better. (But he had only been a little over six then.)

When he danced the plank-one-step, he always hoped he was dancing without an audience. Fishing was good, he rationalized, each time he took the one step backwards. Yes it was good, on this side of the boatlocks. That's where his uncles caught most of their fish! Wasn't it?

The Boy's Father-Uncle Charlie didn't like the fact that one of his posts was at the west end of the plank and another was at the east. He caught a lot of fish in both of these spots.

He didn't like it because, "ga-dammit," he had to field questions from every "f-fisherman" from the west side of town. They troubled him both coming and going. There was no escape for Uncle Charlie. On weekends and holidays, one might hear more protesting Charlie-grunts and grumble-growls than rumblings from the Old Dam.

These two Charlie-posts required grunts, yes, required them. "Scab" grunts or "Nope, not today" grunts. Or, when fishing was really good "Ya-ah. Bitin' last week." He had the perfect Tonto-talk answers for a Scab. Perfectly chewed, chopped, lost, or thrown, or hidden words, but no answer at all was his most commonly perfect poem. His kind of perfection required no smile. Eye contact was out of the question.

"Rookie!" was the only word Charlie enunciated from the head of his boatlocks. "Rookie!" was issued with malice whenever another fisherman lost a fish, or got a snag, or experienced some other defeugalty. "Rookie" was issued often. No one else had previously owned so much of that word.

All this trouble befell an uncle who didn't want trouble. He wanted no impositions. None what-so-ever. He didn't want to react to the impositions either. He didn't want to give up even one grunt. He would rather put his grunts in a bank and collect interest on them. Each syllable was a valuable asset.

Interspersed between grunts and "Rookie"(s), Charlie's slight-of-hand act was being performed at his minnow pail. He caught many fish and didn't want the other fishermen to know about a single one. This, of course, he couldn't accomplish. But, those fishermen had no idea just how many he did catch. If they had, Charlie would have been covered with Scabs. When Charlie made the most catches, the Scabs missed them. Each catch was a secret not to blab about. Charlie then hid the fish between the top and bottom sections of his minnow pail. Sometimes, somehow, there would be ten fish caught before the Scabs were aware of a single bite. This became a family legend, told often. The Boy never tired of it. Few outsiders were clever enough to witness this magic act. Uncle Charlie was good.

He deserved his reputation and his billing. When the fish circus was in town, he was billed as, simply, Chuck, Chas, Grunt, Grumble, Charles, Chink, Hump, Hunker, Chunk, Chocolate, or as Boatlocks-Charlie or First-pier-peer. Had the Boy been asked to bill the magician, he would have succinctly put UNCLE CHARLIE in bright lights.

The Boy didn't like the one-step, but he continued to dance it.

When he wasn't dancing, he did occasionally catch a fish. When he did so, he inevitably showed it to everyone he could. Once, while showing his catfish, it flopped, scaring him into dropping it back into the boatlocks. Most fish he caught, however, completed his boatlock show-and-tell parade.

The Boy then ran home for another showing there, with a "Hey Leo, look at this one," along the way.

The Boy couldn't be blamed that April and May then became June as he continued to practice the one-step. The two-step did, finally follow slowly, but it did follow in a ponderous cadence.

During this time, The Boy reasoned that some of the fishermen he saw did not come from the west side. "How did they get out there on the dam?" he questioned.

So, he proceeded by deduction. By merely crossing the long F Avenue Bridge, he found that he could walk around the Bue-Pain Gas Company where his Aunt Frances worked. Then by doubling back, and by merely tramping over the steel grates above the millrace, the Boy could get to the steps that rose up to the dam. And by merely climbing those steps and hiking all the way across the entire length of the long dam, he could come to the steps on the boatlock end of the dam. From there it was a breeze to slide down the smooth hand-rail on the steps over the fish ladder. Then, there he was, at the foot of the boatlocks. Now all that was required was to waltz, to hop-step, to the head of the locks. Having accomplished that, he arrived at the opposite end of the plank. The Boy was just a little dizzy. But he had arrived at his destination where his uncle stood at his eastern post, grunting.

The Boy soon became a fixture at the Old Dam. His relationship with the plank became well known. His circuitous route introduced him to every fisherman in the vicinity. They showed him their catch. Taught him new secrets. It revealed many aspects of the personalities of the Old Dam's relatives. The Boy liked what he was learning.

With all this new knowledge, the Boy began to "catch" fish every day. Caught them as a result of the fact that the fishermen didn't want to "mess with just one fish." So, since they had grown to like the Boy, they gave their single catches to him. Some days, he caught two fish, some days four. Once, when he walked his route three times, he "caught" his limit, without catching a single fish.

At first, his mother was very proud. Second, his father grew suspicious.

Third and last, his Uncle Charlie, who always knew, grunted to his parents.

THE 38 POUNDER

Into July the Boy was still anticipating. When that had started back in April, his skin had been as white as maggots. Now he was a dark mudcat brown. He was very ribby but not potbellied like a muddy. The Boy weighed almost the same as the "thirty-eight pound" mudcat his uncle had caught in the high water the week before. (When they weren't biting, of course.)

Charlie had hooked a sunfish. He cut off the spines of its dorsal fin and used the whole fish for bait.

An unusual kind of Uncle Charlie's magic began. Everyone saw this show—from the dam, from the bridge, from the western canyon rim. The fish fought for a half hour and thirty-eight minutes.

The Old Calcutta took on a fantastic bend as the fish battled.

Some speculated that it was a snag. Others bet that it was a King Carp. The mudcat had swallowed the hook, fish, and sinker. Its mouth was enormous, its jaws powerful. With his uncle's help the Boy pried the mouth open and put a stick in to hold it opened. The stick was over fifteen inches long. The Boy shuddered at a thought of what such an open mouth could swallow.

Uncle Charlie's hand was usually large enough to hold a catfish head in one hand as he cleaned it. He'd hook his thumb and index finger around each of the two side-horns. In that position he made a quick shallow cut through the skin around the base of the fish's head. Then he cut a little slit down toward the top horn. Where the two cuts joined to make a T, Charlie pulled the skin down with his pliers. Usually the cats were so slippery that the pliers wouldn't hold. It took several grips to remove all the skin. The Boy liked to watch this part because he thought the fish were also beautiful without the skin. The flesh looked whiter, the tail and fins looked darker. At this point in the cleaning, Charlie turned the fish around and pulled up on the little white bib of skin on the upper-underbelly. With his left hand still holding the head, he gripped the body of the fish with his right hand and strangled the fish in a twisting motion that broke the backbone. It also sometimes popped one of the bladders. With a final pull most of the guts came off with the head. All that remained to be done was a final cut through anus and belly. Charlie "didn't do no fin or tail cuttin," that was "homework."

The Boy's mother could always identify a Charlie-cleaned fish. She insisted that if Charlie gave him fish to bring home, the Boy should first remove the fins and the tail. He also should cut off that ugly neck bone where part of the white bladder stuck. The Boy could easily tell what the importance of the last instruction was, by his mother's volume and intonation, as she pointed at the fish. "Make two cuts so that you are sure to remove all of the vent."

The "thirty-eight pounder's" head was too big for Uncle Charlie's usual method. Charlie had to drive a spike through its head and into a telephone pole so he could clean it.

The Boy's Grand grandmother proclaimed a celebration at her house. The Boy could even stay overnight.

That fish was "goo-ood!" Gramma had cooked it so nice and crispy that "Grampa liked it out loud." The Boy's grandmother was surprised at that. (Nona Ruby, the Boy's mother, cooked a meatloaf for his father, who still didn't like no fish.)

The spirit of the "thirty-eight pounder" was now the spirit of the family. The generations moved from the kitchen into the dining room, where there was no dining unless it was Christmas or Thanksgiving. They sat around the oak table with its minnow net tablecloth.

Into the conversation swam a family wordplay, a communion, a repeating nomenclature in honor of the fish they had eaten. It swam from the bellies of the family into their bloodstreams, their hearts and their minds. And in the swimming, swam a song, then songs. The signatures of the songs were the Old Dam, the Boatlocks and many fish, Family-Fish.

Pout, pups, bull and mudpups. Cat, cats, channel and blue. Blue-channel and mudcat catfish fish. Pouch and Bullpouch. Bulls, bullies and yellow-bellies. Bull pout pups. Muddies and Flat-heads. Pout, pups, bull and mudpups...

Later when the Boy was in bed almost asleep, he could still hear "...then I could see the Old Calcutta bending way down..."

And later still, when he was awakened by his uncle's loud snoring, he was surprised to learn that his uncle even grunted "Rookies" in his snores.

No, certainly not. The words that came from Charlie on the day of the "thirty-eight pounder" were not an echo of the words Charlie used when he was at his post. These words could never be extruded from the mouth of Uncle Charlie when he was on duty. The wordplay songs were communion hymns. They were sung after a beer, or two. A sentence, a whole sentence, from Charlie was so rare.... The wordplay-words were family. Family-Words.

When Charlie fished his western post he was somewhat like a red-winged blackbird. The Boy could see those birds in the willows, on the riverbank, upstream. Both Charlie and the birds owned the property on which they stood. They both cast threatening shadows. When necessary, they each could get exactly between the sun and the Boy, making the Boy very uncomfortable with their hovering. One of Father-Uncle Charlie's jackets had epaulettes on the shoulders. The red slashes on the wings of the birds seemed to indicate that the birds had served in a war, too. Both had flat voices. Charlie's was a grumble. It's true. But he could blackbird-scold, in his grumble, too. They both fiercely defended their territories.

The Boy wondered. He wondered what birds his other relatives were. Uncle Will would be a robin, but he didn't fish with worms. He used three, or even four minnows, all hooked on at the same time, or stink bait. Maybe he was a sea gull. "What bird am I?" the Boy wondered. Continuing, he thought, "If I was a pigeon I could fly to the other side of the plank."

Sometimes Charlie hunkered down at his post. He did that often enough so that the other fishermen knew him in that position. It was as if he were part of the earth itself. Quite often he hunkered down with one foot on the plank and the other one on the concrete. This gave Charlie a better angle for fishing exactly in the corner below the falls. When he hunkered there, he was a Charlie, a wood Chuck, a ground Hog, who wouldn't yield an inch.

He wouldn't budge when a fisherman came to walk the plank. In Charlie's position, there was no way the fishermen could hear his grunted answer to their questions. If there was a Charlie answer. Or question. Question? From Charlie? "Huh!" Everyone knew that Charlie was bereft of questions! Perhaps bereaving.

The fishermen had to slide past, to step over, and around, the earthen Charlie, in order to cross the plank. The Boy watched. Who <u>was</u> Charlie?

Crappies liked to tease the father-uncle. He'd have the Old Calcutta pointed straight down toward the corner of the boatlocks. As straight down, that is, as he could with that big bend in the Old Calcutta. Below, in that corner's foam, you might see Charlie's cork. It was small. Shellaced. It was the same color as the Old Calcutta. The cork had a stick through it. The stick had a single-hitch knot tied above the cork and a double-hitch tied below. This engineering enabled Uncle Charlie to manipulate his cork like a puppet.

About six inches down, there was a six-pound-test leader with a small split-shot sinker. Charlie's hook had a long shank and a narrow curve. (Charlie sharpened the hook's barb often.)

To ensure the greatest action, a crappie minnie was hooked between its backbone and its dorsal fin or sometimes through the lips.

If Charlie thought he might have a bite, he would ease the cork up, out of the water. From that position, he felt the line for signals from the fish, nibbles and nobbles. Fish signaled Charlie often. Sometimes he would lift the "kirk" so high that you could see a crappie chase the minnow right up to the surface. The flash and the swirl were beauty-full.

The Boy had to be content with fishing downstream from his Uncle Charlie. His fear of the plank was responsible for this contentment. He also had to accept fishing directly across from one of his Uncle Will's favey-favorite spots.

"Fishing" was throwing rocks too, or teasing the painted or the leatherback turtles. Making frogs jump was fun. Backing crawdads was great.

THE BOATLOCKS

When the Boy was eight, he didn't know anything about the original reason for the boatlocks. It had been years since a boat had passed through them. (One wonders if a boat ever did.) The Boy didn't even imagine such a thing. The place-name "boatlocks" and "boats" never even connected for him.

One of the original steel locks, which had been designed to raise the water, had fallen off the east wall. It fell to the west side of the boatlocks and caused a current to rush around it. There at the end of that rusted metal artifact was Uncle Will's post. He caught blue and channel catfish there, especially when the river began to rise.

The Boy fished, leaning on a railing, where the remaining lock still stood. From there he was a throw-in-the-line-and-move-it boy, a very-very boy "fisherman." He didn't catch many. Sometimes he caught Uncle Will's line, though. Thank God, it wasn't Uncle Charlie's!

Once, in a flash, the Boy saw a chipmunk—or was it one of the river rats?—go down between the concrete wall and the standing metal lock. It wasn't long before the Boy's territory expanded. He learned how to scurry down and up the lock wall like a chiprat. He could make all the sounds one made, too.

During a time when the water was quite low, he climbed down and learned how to stretch-search way out with his foot, for the fallen lock. Then he step, step-walked on the ribs of the "sunken ship."

From there he did quite a bit of fishin'. Mostly, however, he unhooked the snags, down there—for his fishing friends. While the Boy did these boy things, he did of course, think boy thoughts. Not the least of these was how lucky he was to be the youngest boy at the boatlocks. And even beyond that, how lucky he was because he was almost-always, the only boy at the boatlocks.

THE VICTORY

On August 5th, amid his one-day-at-a-time countdown until that year's first day of school, the Boy had his half birthday. He was now eight-and-a-half! "Eight-and-a-half!" he told everyone. "Eight-and-a-half!"

At the boatlocks he found several fishermen. He told the two, who were on his side, all about it.

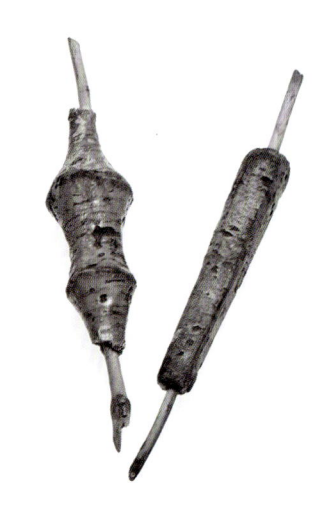

Then he walked directly to the plank and step...step... step-step, he step-walk walked and gave a little run.

He was on the other side!

He hadn't completely learned the fox, the trot, yet. But he had walked the plank.

"I'm eight-and-a-half now and I can walk the plank." He didn't just say it; he was eight-and-a-half—he sang and jumped and danced it, choreographed it!

From his Uncle Charlie's eastern post, under his breath the Boy grunted, "I'm a little dizzy now," but only the Old Dam was listening.

THE RACE

As winters wore on, the Boy needed no reminders what-so-ever to tell him that late April would mean good fishing.

From his perfect-sized desk in grade school, one of the smallest in the room, the Boy began to lean toward the Old Dam in February.

Up until then basketball seemed to have saved him. Tided him over winter's hump. It was as if magnetic gods took turns attracting the Boy's attention. Now fate, wearing fishing gear, loomed ahead of him enormously.

Before he could fish, though, he must first endure a painful period of waiting, seasoned with teasing.

Part of that teasing involved his wait for the return of the red-winged blackbirds. The Boy's mother kept a record of the dates they returned each year. She marked the days on her calendar. Last year it was early. (March 2nd) The year before was average. (March 5th) This year the Ides of March came and left without disaster. April Fool's Day approached but the blackbirds did not arrive.

The Boy's March walks to the Old Dam were only practice sessions. The water was snow-melt high.

35

Then the real season seemed to begin as the water cleared. The blackbirds arrived, insulated in the warmth of their own songs. The Old Dam's ankles reappeared. But the icy fingers of April-dawn persisted along the catwalks. The Boy's depleted patience disappeared. His school days doubled and tripled in length.

Finally, as if in a direct response to the Boy's exhausted wishes, the days did lengthen—lengthened like a tide of light rushing up the Boy's Cedar River. Day and night finally arrived at their annual agreement to keep old promises of rhythmic change.

The sun warmed the Boy's face. The maggot-white pall of winter began to be overtaken by the beginning of his mudcat tan.

The Boy's thoughts were not linear. From his little desk at Fillmore, he could project himself anywhere. At 3:10 school would be dismissed. It might as well have been 1:10, or even earlier, because at about that time the Boy released his imagination on a fine April day.

The Old Dam was eight blocks from the school. The Boy's house, his old clothes, and his fish pole were about seven blocks away.

At exactly 3:10 the Boy rose from his seat and broke a school rule. He used the school's fire escape, its shoot-y-chute, to catapult himself from the school's lack of fire. He landed on his feet, running.

The Boy was determined to set a new record for arrival at the Old Dam. And in doing so, he would keep the promise he had made. He wasn't sure who he had made the promise to, but he had vowed to run everywhere he went. Or at least, he would run two blocks to every one that he walked. He had heard a hint about this kind of dedication from Sam Cooper. Mr. Cooper coached the "kid," the "fox," the "trot," at the school. Yes, he would keep that promise, the Boy thought. Yes he would!

It was easy for this boy to keep this promise. In fact the magnet that was the Old Dam had a huge positive attraction for running, a negative disposition for strolling. How could the Boy creep when he could fly?

He had to run and he had to pant, too. He panted especially hard when he passed someone on the sidewalk. It was also effective to pant when he got home, while changing clothes. The Boy wanted to make sure that his mother could properly evaluate his urgency. A display of physical energy like panting was by far more expressive and immediate than any words he knew how to choose.

In order to keep his appointment with the Old Dam, he knew he must use his most physical and mental alertness.

His mother knew exactly what he wanted. She helped him hurry, but she was his mother and she was not beyond teasing. "Leo's got some new marbles..." she trailed off...

From his house to the dam, laden with a tackle box, pole, brown paper bag, a special handkerchief, and bait, he neither walked nor ran. He shuffle-danced, a necessary compromise. "Damn-it," he had learned, and he smiled it to himself as he scissored along. As he saw how he looked in Scolaro's store window, he exaggerated his shuffle-dance so that others might see. His tackle box banged his leg adding rhythm. The tip of his pole scraped the cement, zip-zip, zip. Some of is worms and their dirt danced out of their can.

The Boy was dancing in a transition between his school and his Old Dam.

When he rounded the lumberyard and arrived at the Old Dam, he discovered that he had finally won the race—he had beaten his uncles. They got off work at 3:30. But _they_ had cars. _Their_ mothers didn't slow _them_ down with kisses. _They_ didn't change clothes. Why did _he_ have to carry that brown paper bag? Yet, he _did_ win. _He_ got to the dam first, he bragged within the Old Dam's hearing.

When Uncle Charlie and Uncle Will arrived minutes later, they _did_ hear the details of his victory. But he hadn't taken their posts. He knew better than that! The probable Uncle Will "Weenie!" or the certain Uncle Charlie "Scab!" he could do without.

The Boy caught the first fish. He was casting. Trying to alarm the painted turtle sleeping in the sun on the fallen lock. His reel backlashed into an all-too-familiar knot. The Boy was poor at untangling such defeugalties. By the time the line was ready, a catfish had caught itself by swallowing the hook.

The Boy was very surprised when the fight began. He was still thinking painted turtles.

Twice the fish caused the line to snag on the lock. Each time it was the fish that freed the line by swimming in the opposite direction. The Boy took credit for both successes.

He tried reeling in the catfish, as he had with smaller versions. Each time the Boy tried this, the fish would make a run. The handles on the reel slapped his fingers as it spun backwards.

This guy was too heavy! The Boy wasn't strong enough to crank him up even after the fish grew tired. He was so excited that the only solution was decided by the action of his feet. He began backing up. He saw the fish rise from the water but as he backed, the Boy could no longer see the fish. Yet, he could feel its weight. He still had him!

The line scraped dangerously over the sharp concrete edge of the locks as he backed up. The tip of the pole was not held high, as he had been taught to hold it. Because of the weight of the fish, the eye of the pole pointed directly toward the rim of the boatlocks. All the strain from the fish pulled directly on the line now.

The Boy's back was approaching the "Dam Site" sign. Then, the line stretched dangerously. Something was caught. The Boy pulled harder. The fish flew over the edge in a wide arc, causing the Boy to fall backwards. His recovery was immediate. He was on the fish in an instant. He pinned it to the cinders. The fish was his! Its horns had only stung him once.

"And, And..." the Boy kept saying. "And look how big it is! Wow!"

He measured it on the fifteen inch ruler painted on top of his tackle box. The fish was longer than the box. He carefully marked with a finger that spot on its tail that went beyond the box. He measured it several times. Each time the fish got bigger. (Did the whiskers count? Could the tail be stretched? Could the belly be flattened?) He searched for someone with a scale. He guessed at its weight. The uncles nodded.

The Boy declared that the channel catfish was sixteen and... (He wanted to know what those little lines between the inches were.) The Boy declared that the channel catfish was sixteen and five-eighths inches long. He declared this as if he knew, and had always known, what five-eighths of an inch was. He wanted his Uncle Charlie to guess that the fish weighed ten pounds. He even had the audacity to ask if perhaps it wasn't five ninths or six tenths or seven elevenths of an inch. The uncles nodded. Charlie grumbled something and pulled up his line. He moved to another spot. "Well?"... the Boy asked Will, who nodded but didn't answer... the Boy looked up, again, surprised, to see if Will was turning into Charlie. Reassured, the Boy continued, "Well, tenths are bigger than ninths aren't they?" The grunt he heard from Will was alarming.

He returned to the safe occupation of fish admiration.

He eventually took the chain stringer out of his tackle box. After several tries he was able to close the snap on the stringer that secured the fish. His hands still shook with nervous excitement.

Charlie had taught him how to string a catfish. Most fishermen put the stringer through the gill and out the mouth. Charlie, however, forced the sharp point of the snap right through the head and the lower jaw of the fish, near its lips.

The Boy was so proud of this fish that he used Charlie's technique with one snap, and for security reasons, he applied the usual method with a second snap. The fish hung at a limp curving angle, when it had floppd its last flopping.

The Boy continued pulling the fish out of the water, at short intervals, to show passing fishermen and to reassure himself that it had not escaped.

He also pulled it in, hand over hand, all the way up to the top of the boatlocks, several times, just to admire it.

The beauty of the fish, in raking light, burned into the Boy's mind. Later in his life, he would remember that specific fish and its radiance. He would also acquire a composite sense of beauty from all fish. (Later, the Boy, as a young man, would in a moment of passion, admire the inside of the left forearm of his wife-to-be. He told her that her arm, with its color and its young springtime freckles, looked like "...an April channel catfish," the most beautiful thing in the world. She gave him an unexpected response, the old cold fish.)

Pulling the fish out of the water so many times took a toll on the sixteen and five eighths incher. So did the way the Boy had strung it.

By 6:30 he carried the fish. Now more than aesthetics were wanting.

In a small sphere of sadness the Boy drug himself and the dead fish over behind the Farmer's Market. He was going to clean it. His arm, which had been proudly holding the stiff cadaver in front of him, dropped to his side.

The sounds of the traffic and the water, in fact all his peripheral perceptions, retreated into the work of cleaning the fish.

He even remembered to remove the long dark line of matter along the backbone. According to his mother's instructions, he scraped his fingernail, hard, over each of those bones to make it blood free. (It was the fish's liver he had been told.) If it was not carefully removed the fish would not taste as good at supper. The Boy grinned. He could hear his father saying, "That fish won't taste anything at supper. He's kaput. The last thing that fish tasted was a worm. You can taste that fish. I want a ham-mur-mer."

His father's humor served as an encouragement for the Boy to scrape the backbone even harder. As he did so, he noticed that the fish shivered. He wondered how a dead fish could quiver like that? He also wondered what made him shiver when the fish did?

Then he remembered the dog fish, the one that Moose Maudsley had caught recently at the dam. The Moose had cussed as soon as he saw it. He thought he had caught a game fish. All during the fight Moose kept imagining a huge northern pike, because the dog didn't fight like a cat, or a carp. It was a real fight! The Boy considered himself lucky to have seen it. Garnished with other spicy words, Moose Maudsley kept saying, "Ga-damn ga-dogfish, a dog fish—ga-dogfish—damn a big old dog fish fish."

Nearly running out of creative expletives, but still energetic and angry, the Moose cut the heart out of the still fighting fossil. Moose Maudsley then peed in his fish-worm can and threw the heart in.

Spitting, "Piss on it, little man," Moose Maudsley stomp-ted home.

Moose had caught the big dog from the top of the dam between the fifth and sixth pier. To the Boy, short as he was, this place was a trench. His view was concrete, three sides of concrete, with a sky for a ceiling. It was just wide enough for two men to pass each other. (Providing they were not both wearing pup tents.) There were a few holes in the floor. Through these the Boy could see the water rushing over the dam.

Quillback, redhorse, and carp, at various stages of decay, lay rejected where the men had thrown them.

It was a room too small for noses.

Fishermen would boost themselves up to sit and fish from the top of the dam. This, the Boy could not yet do. But he did, often, stand on his upright tackle box and peek over. Even in this security, he felt a little dizzy. It was a full twenty-five feet down to the surface of the river.

Three days later, the Boy saw the heart, still beating, in the can. He never forgot the miracle of the heart or the combined stink of the dead worms, and the piss. The Boy pronounced that last word just exactly as Moose Maudsley had.

By the fourth day the heart had stopped beating but the stink was palpitating. The heart floated on top of several dreadful colors that drew the Boy's attention.

He could see that the heart <u>did</u> still move but not in the same way it had. The Boy's usual curiosity drew him closer, in spite of the putrid obstacles.

Upon even closer investigation, he saw that the slow movement was caused by his old acquaintance, Boiling Rice.

From his fishing perch, Gill Caggle saw the Boy's scrutinizing fascination. He said, leaping down, "Watch this." Gill then took a saltshaker from his tackle box. He sprinkled salt on the heart.

The Boy was amazed. The heart started beating again. Then the maggots and the heart appeared to have chosen to dance by themselves.

They certainly weren't dancing to the same rhythm. Losing heart, the accelerating maggots shriveled into a salty frenzy.

As the Boy watched, the heart lost heart too: the dance ended. "Kaput," said the Boy, just exactly as his father had. "Kaput." He had said it once for the heart of the dogfish. (That very persistent heart.) He had said it a second time for the maggots. "Kaput," he said again, this time for the sheer pleasure and finality of the word itself.

So, out of a memory, and out of the completion of his fish cleaning, the sounds around the Boy returned. His fishy hands swatted the places where the first mosquitoes buzzed. He warshed his hands in the river. It was cold. He was a boy. He didn't wash too carefully.

He returned to the dam, the cleaned fish in a bread wrapper inside the brown paper bag. (His mother had been right. Again.)

Each of the uncles had caught crappies and catfish. They fished until the long workday took its toll on them. Frances would have dinner ready for Uncle Will. He would play with Larry and Judy, and with baby Jim. Charlie would enjoy one of the home brews his mother made.

Before they left, the Boy heard them discussing the lengthening of the days. The uncles agreed that it was spring-change that made them happy. But, these days, they thought, demanded more...

When the sun also tired from its longer daily struggle, it lay down on the rippling water below the Old Dam. It gently floated under the F Avenue Bridge. Through an arch of the bridge the Boy could see the sun's orange glow retreat slowly down to the First Avenue Bridge. The buildings along the east bank of the river all looked new in this light, having been freshly painted by the drifting sun. (The pride of the city, the Veterans Memorial Coliseum, became a glowing torch. It was grander than any of the expectations of her artists. It was a tower of sunset glory, a torch of thanks to those who gave their lives for our freedom.)

As the sun drifted to the next bridge, its light seemed to begin to rise up from the river. At the Third Avenue Bridge it reached the switch; it turned on the night lights of all the bridges.

This marked the moment, the division, between day and night.

The magic continued. The ripples, now bereft of their sun, became a million bridge lights.

The dam, with no lights at all, was aglow from the shimmering reflections of the waves.

Thousands of bugs began to hum goodnight, as if it were goodmorning. Hundreds rose, on some orchestrated cue, and flew into the small rooms that became the bridge's moons.

The Boy then saw a single magnificent treasure that marked the end of the teasing season, a Luna moth. Its green body-flutter and mysterious wing-ed eyes seemed to wink, and wink at the Boy. It drew him to the moth just as the moth is drawn to the light.

Above the Boy the sounds of the zink birds became evenly spaced. "Zink, zink," they sang... "Zink!"

The Boy was transfixed. He seemed complete. He drifted in a smile.

THE ZINKERS

Finally, he gathered all his things and walked over behind the Farmer's Market again.

He climbed down the bank and sat on one of the limestone rocks. He leaned back against another. A perfect chair, he thought. He liked to watch the way the lights gave extra life to the current as it came down from the F Avenue Bridge.

The Boy was very quiet. Out of the corner of his eye he saw a rat emerge from the Vinton Ditch. It drifted like a boat, its legs somewhere in the darkness, into a hole between two limestones. Worried, the Boy put his fish into the tackle box. He sat back again, ready to receive and interpret the night.

The zink birds flew their rhythmic flight in and out of the F Avenue Bridge's lights to the Boy's left. To his right, they did the same at the First Avenue Bridge. The island looked like a boat emerging upstream out of the bridge and the night.

The powerhouse, across the river laid down a quiet hum from its turbines, generating and sending their own personal light through the small panes of its large windows.

"Zink, zink." The birds climbed until they saw an insect far below. The Boy never tired of watching the dives and the restless flight of the zinkers. He hoped that they didn't eat Luna moths.

He drifted. The Boy wondered what his punishment would be for shooting the shoot-y-chute. He hoped he wouldn't have to stay after school again. He didn't want to write on the blackboard again. That would be terrible, unless it was raining hard, or if the fish quit biting.

In that event, he wouldn't mind staying after school at all. He liked his teachers.

He drifted further. If he ever had the opportunity to teach his teachers a lesson, he thought, he'd make them learn the multiplication tables of the insects at the Old Dam, the division of day and night, the addition of fish on a stringer and the subtraction of the big ones that got away. He'd teach the poems of Moo - Moose - Maud - Maudsley. That's what he'd do! He would!

>   Zink zink zinkbird
>   Zink zink zinker
>   A Zinker sinker
>
>   Dogs and cats
>   Dogs and catfish fight
>   Cats and dogfish fish
>
>   Bats bite at night
>   On a hip pocket kite
>
>   Zink zink stinker

The Boy smiled as his mind returned to his river. He watched the dives of the zinkbirds. The low sound of stress produced on the wings of the birds as they pulled out of a dive was his favey-favorite sound in nature. (His favey-favorite collections were full of such favey-favorites.)

The bridges, the power plant, the limestone wall, and the upper limits of the lights in low clouds, formed the ceiling and the walls of a living room for the Boy.

By now, the little sisters of the rat were flying out of their cave into his living room. The bats lived, by the thousands, in the cave that was the Vinton Ditch.

Vinton is a town northwest of the Red Cedar rapids. The Boy knew that detail. From where he sat he could see the mouth of the Ditch. The roof of the mouth was a carefully constructed arch of bricks. This mouth smiled in the daylight. The Boy wasn't sure about its demeanor at night. But, it appeared to be friendly, even in the dimness of his room that was never completely dark.

The cave continues in the same configuration where the mouth becomes the throat, where the throat becomes the intestines where the intestines become the...

At the other end of the Vinton Ditch, near Roosevelt School, the cave emerges to become an actual ditch that parallels E Avenue.

The Boy knew that the Vinton Ditch drew its water from the meandering creek (which the Boy pronounced crick.) to the northwest. From that point, and upstream, the creek was alive with minnies, with crawdads and with green leopards.

The great number of bats now darkened his room. They made it nervous with their flight.

The Boy reached for his fish pole. He took off the hook and sinker. He cranked the line all the way into the reel. Then he reached into his left sock where he had tucked his special handkerchief. This he carefully tied on to the eye-tip of his pole.

He gripped the handle with both hands. He lifted it as high as he could.

The Boy whipped the hanky through the air while he watched the bats swarm and dart around his "insect." It was the birth of a ritual.

He became his pocket-handkerchief. He was the loony moth that every bat desired but none could catch.

He lost his energy at the same time the bats lost their interest. He, almost, zinked himself to sleep in a lullaby of nighthawks.

The Boy patted his tackle box and lugged his treasures home.

Nona Ruby acted perturbed because the Boy was so late. Frank Lester nodded in agreement. Both parents soon entered into the Boy's excitement, though, as he shared <u>most</u> of the highlights of his day.

His father said he missed playing catch with the Boy. He insisted that the Boy take a bath.

The last thing the Boy remembered before he went to sleep was the taste and the smell of the fish-cleaning that still lingered on the thumb he was sucking.

His loony-moth dream that night was of the alchemy of salt. He dreamed that he was a teacher, teaching his teachers. His classroom was his living room, between the bridges.

He was telling how the gold in salt could awaken the dead and kill the living.

But only the Old Dam was listening.

THE ACT OF HOOKY

The Boy did not receive capital punishment for shooting the shoot-y-chute. In fact, no one had seen him do it except Miss Darling, the Boy's teacher. She was from the roots of an old family tree of teachers. Miss Darling might have been ancient Athena's very great-granddaughter. In the Boy's eyes she was certainly a goddess.

She had what she thought was a secret admiration for the Boy.

She decided that if the Boy didn't repeat his performance, she would forget it.

Now, Ronnie Young and Leo Hejda also knew about the shoot-y-chute shot. Walking to school the boys had talked it over, and over. None of them thought it would be worth shooting again, unless of course, they could all do it together. Each of them knew that Ronnie wouldn't do it if it involved a possibility of losing reading time.

Only Ronnie knew that he could have even more exciting adventures in books.

Leo wouldn't do it for Leo reasons. Nobody, not even Leo, understood Leo reasons. Never-the-less, they all knew Leo wouldn't take a shot at the chute without the others but he pree-intended he might.

47

As they crossed the CNW RR tracks, where the street took a slight turn to the right, Leo detonated an enormous fart.

Ronnie and the Boy laughed and protested. Leo was proud. He laughed the hardest. Leo laughed just over the verge of laughing too hard.

Farts were one of their favey-favorite subject matters. They went into great detail comparing this particular success to the odors so familiar near the Cedar rapids.

Rapidians said they could read the direction of the wind by sniffing. That day, the breeze was from the southeast, from the Penny-kin-Ford plant, where they made cornstarch and syrup from corn. Where the trains rumbled out with bottles and boxes of good food. Where what was left, was the likes of The Leo.

Yes, Ronnie carefully read the breeze, and from his little mouth, he confirmed that "The Leo Wind was a perfect approx-im-ation of the fur-for-all plant at Quaker's."

With that pronouncement, they all laughed again. Ronnie laughed the loudest. He was so proud that he overstepped his audience with, "We have a fas-ination with flat-ulation." No one laughed.

All the boys agreed that The Leo wasn't anything compared to the heavyweight of winds—especially the one from Wilson's Packing Plant that hung over the city on a hot summer day.

Leo vowed to try harder. "Don't brown your drawers" chimed the others. They discussed what should be eaten for better quality control. Sauerkraut and Spam over smashed but-tate-uls was the consensus as they arrived at Fillmore.

Fillmore. If asked, it was school in general, that the boys vowed they hated. But Fillmore? Fillmore they loved! And if the truth were known, even school in general was sacred.

It was a place where the family and the neighborhood and the world were emancipated. It was a place where life relaxed while being offered the opportunity for endless adventure. So, Fillmore would have been a temple if it had a gym.

Fillmore's archive stood ready. Ready daily to expand the kids who entered it.

The changes achieved, however, were usually not the ones planned by the dults. The Boy had misunderstood the word adult. He heard it as "a dult." He thought that meant one dult.

Dults were gods.

At Fillmore there were many female dults, the teachers. There was only one male, the prince-ipal dult.

The building was already full of dults when the boys arrived each morning. It was also full when they left. Even when they came for conferences, it was full of dults. These facts conjured many images in the boys' heads.

The old quarried-stone school sat in the middle of the block. In spots, some couragcous, or stupid, grass grew in the gravel playground.

The boys glanced at the shoot-y-chute and wondered. Next to it, on the left, was the large glass window. It reached above the second floor where it ended in a graceful arch. Inside the window the boys saw the dauntless Miss Darling ascending the well-worn oak stairs. This sighting roused comments that descended the stairs to the level of humor the boys were on before.

Ronnie reached just inside the door, where the sporting balls were stored and brought out a scuffed volleyball. A game of dodge-ball started. It became increasingly aggressive as more and more kids arrived and joined in. It seemed impossible that such small hands and skinny arms could throw a ball that fast.

Downright hostility seemed imminent when the magic of the resounding bell herded the sheep into Fillmore.

But it was hard to herd the all-sports Fillmore teams that had named themselves and had a fight song—

"We're the Fillmore Smudge Pots,
Smudge Pots are we,
We're the Fillmore Smudge Pots,
Smudging on to victory!
Rah, Rah, Rah, Rah!"

Their school colors were The Pink and The Green, and they would never forget their cheerleaders, Jolene Johnson (rah rah rah) and (oh my goodness!) Shirley Meyers!

As the team entered the sacred halls, dults mouthed, "Walk don't run. Walk!" "No running up the steps! Walk now." "You walk / you walk / You walk now walk...."

In the classroom, Miss Darling said, "Good morning class." A chorus of open beaks beamed, "Good morning Miss Darling."

Then all the students stood, placed their right hands on their hearts and said the Pledge of Alley Gents. They all sat again to listen to Miss Darling read the daily announcements. She then assigned an art project.

The Boy had little interest, even though his teacher explained that students would be able to have their work shown at the Public Library.

The morning passed slowly, except for recess, of course. Whammo-dodge-balls bombarded girls in every corner of the playground. Shirley fell and scraped her elbow. She needed some Ma Cure a Comb from the school's anti septic tank.

After the recess bell started its herding, the dults again repeated their poem.
You walk   You walk   You walk
You walk   You walk   You walk
You walk now walk You walk now walk You walk now walk

You run   You talk   You run
You run   You talk   You run
You do not run   You do not talk   You have no fun

    To the class-rooooom-ss, march!

Of course, the kids knew it by heart. They wondered why the dults had such trouble learning it.

Quiet again reigned in the classroom but the playground nervousness in the small arms and legs remained. It was as if the bell was still ringing in their bodies.

The Boy found a pik-chure of a Redheaded Woodpecker in a classroom magazine. This he copied, in crayon. With some success, according to the bright-eyed Darling Miss.

While making the drawing, the Boy often reached into his pocket. There he had a roll of waxed paper with little dots of candy stuck on it. With his fingernail he loosened the candy and snuck it into his mouth. Sometimes, the paper stuck to the candy. It didn't matter to the Boy. It was good anyway. For some reason the candy tasted better when it was clandestine like that. Snuck like that, in school.

Leo, the observer, leaned toward the Boy and whispered a demand for candy.

When the Boy passed a single dot, Leo fumbled it to the floor. There, the fleet Miss Darling nabbed it! She walked toward her desk and deposited it into the wastepaper basket without comment. Not surprisingly many eyes observed this action. It wasn't beyond the candy seeking fingers of those eyes, to reach into that basket later. The mouths of those eyes intended to punctuate that action with the tasty dot.

Pallas Darling was such a darling for not permitting the Boy to pass Leo any more candy.

When Fillmore was out for lunch, its playground again dodged from WHAMMO-balls.

Again, the kids were herded in, again. "This is a magnificent cerulean day." That's what the dults said to each other while interrupting their own "You walk / You walk / You walk don't run." pome.

It was the sunniest and the warmiest day of the young year. The burr oak leaves were the size of squirrel's ears. Uncle Charlie knew how to read tree leaves. He had read them aloud to the Boy. But the Boy couldn't remember if crappies bit when hard maples dropped their spinning seeds, or if it was that carp bit then. Did crappies bite when the basswood were in bloom? Squirrel's ears? He promised himself that he would listen more carefully the next time.

It was definitely a hooky day. Hooky! What a word. Hooky, a word kids liked to play with. A word that trembles through kids and dults alike.

The sun came through the window and warmed the Boy's perfectly sized school seat, but not the Boy. The sun was warming the Boy at the Old Dam. The Old Dam was, in turn, warmed by the Boy.

The dam had seemed lonely when the Boy arrived. He wondered if it was always that way during school hours.

That afternoon the dam seemed reluctant to teach the Boy new tricks. But it did offer some baby tadpoles. It showed some moss that was just starting to grow in the fish ladder. It scared the wits out of the Boy when it appeared as an enormous, very stinky, snapping turtle under the F Avenue

Bridge. He left it alone after observing how easily it broke the stick he had poked at it. He looked at his finger for reassurance.

The Old Dam introduced him to several fishermen who worked the night shift. The Boy found a hook, a sinker and their broken line on a snag. He made a noose with the line and failed to catch the chipmunk and the rat that lived in the boatlock. He happily failed at many-many things. But he was successful at starting a summer tan and a mild burn.

The word "hooky" rolled over his mind and over his tongue and over the dam many times. It could be heard best near the plank. It was a word that still had a great feeling of joy mixed into it. It was a word warmed, and a word colded like a popsicle, too.

At 3:15 the Boy went home. He tried to time his arrival perfectly, as if he had just been dismissed from school. He skipped the panting though. He changed his clothes and did his usual doings and went to the Old Dam again. This time he was accompanied with his pole, his bait and his aplomb.

His uncles were already at their posts when he arrived. He had timed it perfectly.

The Boy caught two carp. They had put up a wonderful struggle. He pulled them in, hand-over-hand. The Boy was very proud. He strung them standard fashion. Their mouths were too soft for Charlie-stringing. (Charlie didn't keep no carp!)

One weighed about seven pounds he guessed, with the help of Uncle Will. The Boy tried to act like they were not too heavy for him but they were. Everywhere he went, two tails dragged behind.

Then the Boy heard a sound that always delighted him. It was Mr. Kozberg, driving his horse cart past Vernal Street, singing, "Any rags or junk today? Any junk or…." Mr. Kosberg had made his living doing this for a good many years. He had a garage where he kept his horse on the same block where the Boy's grand gramma and his grand grampa lived.

Uncle Roger lit Mr. Kozberg's furnace on Shabbat.

Finally, past Summer Street, the Boy caught Mr. Kozberg's attention. It was worth catching him, too, because he bought the fish for fifty cents. One the Boy delivered to 419 B Avenue, N.W. where Mrs. Blivas, Mr. Kozberg's daughter, filled the Boy with thank yous and compliments, and, another nickel.

The Boy dropped his equipment at home, gave forty cents to his parents, and feeling rich, ran up F Avenue to Scolaro's Grocery Store.

Inside it was filled with groceries from floor to ceiling. He walked around the big bunch of bananas hanging from the ceiling, past the meat cooler to the icebox. Inside he found a Red Rock Cola (his favey-favorite pop) for four cents.

He put the eleven remaining cents in his pocket promising Phil he would return the bottle. If Mr. Scolaro had been there, the Boy would have had to pay a deposit. He almost left before he decided on a one-cent roll of dots.

On his way home the Boy stopped at Leo's and <u>did</u> share his candy. Leo did have marbles. The Boy relieved Leo of twelve beauties.

Leo protested that the Boy had cheated. He said that the Boy had not kept his knuckles on the ground when he shot. He added that the Boy was using a steely unfairly. Leo insisted that a steely should only be used for lagging. (Leo had gone to a marble tournament at Green Square that afternoon. He'd learned that there were rules.) "Now we gots ruu-uules?" wondered the Boy.

One of the marbles that Leo had lost looked like an eyeball. Leo wanted it back bad. The Boy wouldn't.

Leo said, "I'll tell Darling about the hooky." The Boy made a tight little fist. He shook it at Leo hard.

Leo's bottom lip pouted out. He lowered his head and sucked in air in three quick gasps. In spite of his nearness to tears, he still looked determined to tell.

So, the Boy traded for Leo's last fifteen marbles. All Leo had was his eyeball.

It's blackmail, the Boy thought.

Leo was learning. That was the first time he had gone home with any marbles. It was also the first time he'd gone home with three eye-balls.

Leo and his family had sauerkraut and spam for supper that night, over smashed but-tate-uls. The Boy and his family had sauerkraut and cutted-up boiled ring baloney without skin on their smashed but-tate-uls.

The next morning Ronnie, Leo and the Boy walked to school together again. They walked fast because of a sprinkle that was cleaning Cargill out of the air. There had been thunderous rumbling earlier. The air became as sweet as Quaker Oats.

As they neared the school, the Boy acquired a reluctant gait. He straggled a little behind the others. For this he would have been teased, if it hadn't been raining.

The Fillmore loomed over them, a gray mean looking hulk. Ringing louder than usual, the bell immediately herded them in. "You walk / You walk / You walk fast walk," culled and dult-jolted each and every student body, directly and efficiently, into the respective home rooms.

Right away, the Boy assumed a slumped posture in front of his teacher's desk. He did this before his classmates had a chance to quiet down.

Observing this unusual action, Leo unconsciously sat in the wrong seat, his mouth open, listening. He didn't want to miss a single word of this.

Leo lost some of his physical control as he nervously flipped his eyeball from one hand to the other.

The Boy fixed his eyes on the hole in his right shoe. He examined the dirt on the sock that protruded. These were the things on which he seemed to concentrate. His toenail enlarged a hole in the sock's darning. His mouth began to mumble, barely discernible to Miss Darling, and to Leo, whose ear he was unable to avoid. (He'd get him later.)

He mumbled over the room's din, "My mother had twins last winter. One died. Yesterday afternoon, I had to go to the funeral. But, my other brother is OK."

Miss Darling stood up, walked around her desk and hugged the Boy. For the Boy this hug was painfully long.

This was too much for Leo. Leo dropped his marble and gasped. His eyeball rolled across the floor. Darling picked it up. The eye winked at the emerging wet spot in the front of Leo's pants.

During recess, dear Darling called the Boy's mother to express her personal empathy for the loss of the Boy's sibling and for the family's bereavement.

The Boy's mother was very surprised to find that she had given birth to twins and that she had just attended a funeral. Among other things, she told Miss Darling that the Boy's real baby brother was, indeed, healthy and doing well.

The Boy didn't fish that day! Nor did he fish that week! It was perfectly clear that his parents would not listen to any further appeals on that subject. Hooky tanned the Boy twice. The overall effect was very similar to his Marion grand father's often-repeated words: "Wood warms you twice."

The following week it rained almost constantly. The Boy's anguish, along with the rains, flooded Summer Street. His remorse cascaded down the storm-sewers and filled the Vinton Ditch.

As the river rose, the Old Dam's ankles disappeared. It was up to its neck in turbulence.

The Old Dam was wearing a strong and very determined look.

The Boy mumbled something about hooky, but the Old Dam didn't seem to be listening.

4th St NW from 1st Ave North

110 Lenway, Alyce
112 Hoppe, John
120 Moyer, Raymond
124 Nordman, Dean
128 Bucklin, Velma

A Ave NW Intersects

211 Shultz, Gust	Klopp, Malcom 212
213 Giblin, Emmet	Cornwell, Russell 214
217 Sewell, Chas	Haskins, Kenneth 216
221 Stuhr, John	Wolfe, Ted 220
225 Weinberg, Joe	Thompson, Mary 224
227 Kent, Paul	Schwarz, Lillian 226

B Ave Intersects

303 Lewis, Robt	Memen, Wm 312
307 O'Neill, Gerald	Cook, Lawrence 316
311 Lindahl, Robt	
315 Hansen, Bessie	
317 Ciha, John	

E Ave Intersects

605 Steinbecht, Amelia	Elliott, Hazel 602
609 McNeill, Rivers	Procok, Leo 604
613 Zepperer, Helen	Peterson, Elmer 608
	Reinbrecht, Robt 614

Changes

221 Wood   303 Hale, Speraw
227 Gilliam Ward 307 Shop, Bristsky
216 Elgas   315 Bishop
220 Brown, Ferguson

THE HOARD

The river smiled into fishing depth and clarity just as the school year ended.

"Oozsho" the Boy said many times, "Oozsho!" It was his fondest superlative. One step up from favey-favorite. Oozsho, bare feet and fishing stretched out ahead of him as far as his inner eye could see. Oozsho! Once having coined that word, he wasn't about to let it go unused.

What made this year different from other years was the fact that the Boy's father was to get his first vacation from work. Three big days. With pay.

His mother planned to transplant some wildflowers from High Rock.

His father intended to build a pigeon coop for the Boy. "Not to keep the Boy in," the Boy's father kidded, "It'll be for the birds," he added while playing catch with the Boy.

His father slapped his hand into his leather glove. (He often caught the fastest pitchers, slap, slap-slap, in the Industrial League at Ellis Park, slap. Under the lights, slap.) He slapped the glove again. It was more of a mitten than a glove. All that was left of the original glove was a front and a back piece of hide. Now it was impossible to determine if it had been a catcher's mitt or a first baseman's glove. A hole was hacked in the back of the glove. His father had engineered this so he could stick his longest finger out. His hand was like the leather of the glove. He spit in the glove and pounded it with his right hand. This the Boy watched with glee. He admired the strength he saw in his father's action. His own hand would hurt if he hit it with such gusto. The Boy also liked the smell of the glove; its history spoke in sunshine, sweat, spit, leather and enthusiasm, mixed.

The Boy will be the batboy, his father thought. Maybe he'll get a broken bat. Then I can glue and screw it together for him. I'll make it as good as new.

His mother continued her vacation planning. She would take the Boy to the public library to see the Grant Woods while his father watched the baby. But then, she thought, I won't be able to spend the vacation time with Frank. Perhaps we should all go to the show together? No, that wouldn't work either. It's vacation! We could go to the show any time. But no, the show ends this week. Dismissing the idea of going to see the Woods, she pictured the idea of going, just as if she had gone. Her imagining had convoluted on her. She had arrived at a similar position as Pastor Orville Magnus Running had when in response to an invitation to come to the house for dinner, he had said, "I won't be able to come, but I'll enjoy it as much as if I had."

Those Woods were not woods at all, she laughed in her thoughts, who ever heard of woods growing in a public library?

Granted, those would be crazy Woods, she created for Frank in a continuation of her thinking. She chuckled to herself, then sobered when she remembered his often repeated words, "Nona knows what I want before I want it."

She knew that the Boy was used to this kind of banter. He knew Mr. Wood was a teacher at McKinley High School. He was told about that when he had spotted Grant driving his car around the corner near the F Avenue Bridge. His attention had been drawn to the car by Wood's use of a crazy wooden arm he had sculpted to indicate when he was going to turn left or right.

The plans of the parents went on add-infant-item because the Boy's baby brother would enjoy the vacation, too.

On the first day of the vacation the parents did planned-parent things while the Boy was left to monknee around in the yard.

The side yard groveled in the armpit of the Sanitary Dairy—a huge building made of ubiquitous yellow bricks. The facade seemed hungry. The bricks had already eaten two neighboring homes and seemed on the verge of devouring another—the Boy's. Both Leo's and Ronnie's houses watched the situation from across a street. Ronnie's house used to be able to see the Boy's house, but now it couldn't. All it could see, in that direction, was a paltry sanitary wall. The Sanitary Dairy that had been the Blue Valley Dairy liked the idea of growing into a new name every-so-often. As the neighborhood's capitalistic bully, it wanted change. Change! It wanted to sanitize all of the letters of the Boy's alphabet.

For the Boy, this particular day's monkneeing around involved raking the yard in an area where the pigeon coop was to be built. That was easy.

Then he monkneed with digging, mostly in old clinkers from many furnaces. Then more raking.

Then Leo meandered over. He talked, awhile, about, maybe, going barefoot. He also said the price of Red Rock Cola had gone up to five cents at Scolaro's. Then he talked about the thing he always seemed to discuss lately. The loss of his eyeball. It still hurt him. Finally, the Boy found a stick and drew a circle in the best raked spot. Then Leo lost his marbles and went home, again.

The Boy monkneed around.

He dug some more.

Much to his surprise, a coin appeared in the diggings. He couldn't read it. It wasn't like the pennies, or the nickles, or the dimes, or quarters he spent.

The Boy licked it and wiped it on his pants leg. It still wasn't clean. He put it into his mouth to soak it good. Not wanting to waste any time he started to dig again with Ven Gents. The way the dirt and cinders flew looked like he was being helped by ten devils. He found two more coins just as his parents arrived.

In his anxiousness to show them his finds, he jumped up, immediately swallowing the coin. He ran, choking, to his mom and said, in a lower than usual voice that didn't seem to want to talk, "I found," cough, cough, "a strange treasure," (His dad was pounding him on the back.) "Right over there."

The Boy's mother asked why he was talking so funny and why he was coughing.

The Boy was much more interested in telling about his discovery. "Right over there," he croaked.

Then, upon his mother's insistence, he told about swallowing the wonderful coin. "It might be worth a fortune...." (Now his mother was striking him on the back.)

The Boy's voice returned to normal but his face remained maggots.

The whole family went straight to the doktr. Not the ch-eye-ro-practr, this time, but straight to the doktr.

"Examine his stools…" were the Doctor's very-fast initial words that initiated a slowing and scrambling of the minds of the Boy's parents. "… see if the coin passes naturally. 'If-after-three-days-you-still-haven't-found it in-the-stools,' then report back, 'or, if-there-are-any-other-indications-of,' complications of any kind, 'like-stomach-raising-risings,' shortness, or 'quickness-of-breath' or-fat-teeg, 'before-that-time-should-arise,' remember-not-to-let-him-use-the-regular-toilet, 'otherwise-we-will-not-know-if-anything-has-been' passed. 'Report that immediately back sooner than the former-latter.' In the event that the latter becomes an obstruction of the bowels, we may have to operate."

The Boy clearly heard the doctor say, "We May Have To Operate." He also was aware that he was very short. The rest was a jumble of the scary. Stools and ladders? The Boy wondered, what are my ladders and my stools?

Upon their return to Summer Street all three dug for more coins. The first they found was an Indianhead penny. It was much more beauty-full than an ordinary Lincoln. Then as the excitement rose, they found a Buffalo that was worth a nickel. Nona Ruby hastened to the house and returned with a pickle jar. Into this treasure chest they deposited coins as they found them.

Searching for more coins overcame their interest in individual finds. Each of them found many. The possibilities started to seem unlimited when they found a twenty dollar gold piece. It was small, skinny, and untarnished—as bright as new, although it was slightly worn.

"A hoard. It's a 'cash Hoard,'" his father repeated several times, as if it were a chant, "...a cash Hoard." Each time he said it, he forgot that he had said it before.

Like his father, exactly like his father, the Boy said hoard many times. Then he branched out… into a little po-em like he often did. The Boy's mouth played with the chant and soaked the words good.

It was darkness that kept them from undermining the foundation of the Sanitary. Now, it looked like the brick wall had a mouth. If they dug deeper they might find a chin. Then a neck. It was as if they had dug down to the pockets, the ubi, where the brick wall kept its ubique, its ubiquity, its ubiquitous money.

Although they did not find any more coins in the last hour of digging, the possibility of finding more still hung in the air.

THE MOOSE

Besides, Moose Maudsley came over for a beer. His wife Verna came too, just before Wood Chuck Polansky followed the telephone call's wire directly to Summer Street with his wife Evelyn. The Boy was disappointed that Sandy and the young Would Chuck Wood and especially Dick, one of his favey-favorites were all left home with a sitter. Harry Weizel and Hazel Wiezel and Herold, Bobcat and Katydid Sis Brizendine and Hairy Ballzer all came for Penny Ante poker, too. Moose Maudsley came later with some of the fish he had just caught and cleaned.

Soon the kitchen table was arrayed with brightly colored poker chips, cards, one-dollar bills and various coins, mostly copper.

The kitchen filled with laughter and smoke and stories and much much more smoke and a few more stories.

The Boy was on a coin scrub-a-dub mission in the bathroom. He had three different kinds of soap and two brushes. One was his newfangled toothbrush. He used a song, L - A - V - A, a twenty-mule team, Boraxle, and snow, Ivry Snow to clean the coins. He also tried the salt and the baking soda he used on his teeth, when he was told to do so. To his surprise the heads and the tails of the coins emerged from his scrubb-the-crud rubs.

Almost before he began, he lost one coin down the drain. He ran out to tell his father but happily he found him in a "Just a minute," …just a minute's, I'm too occupied, in an occupation. Sadly, dad was just too busy to receive any confessions. "Oh well, no one will miss one little old coin."

63

During one stage of the coin scrub-a-dub, Moose Maudsley came into the bathroom. He examined some of the coins with one hand while he peed with the other.

The Boy noticed that Moose was a little reckless with each hand. Fearing another coin might be lost, the Boy said, "Be careful."

Moose Maudsley smiled, shook off the last drip, put down the coins, zipped, patted the Boy on the head and said, "Piss on it, little man, that's the way to clean coins."

The Boy's admiration for the Moose grew even larger. He always shared in a way that made the Boy feel like a little dult.

Trying to hold the Moose a little longer, the Boy called out, "You forgot to warsh yur hands."

Moose Maudsley stopped, turned, came back into the bathroom, closed the door, a thing the Boy had never seen the Moose do before, leaned close to the Boy, breathed antiseptically into his face, and said, "Moose don't piss on their hands."

Moose jolted his smile back to his cards and his drink, a Sea-Gram-Seven-Seven. (Moose brought his own wisss-key.)

The Boy finished washing the coins. Some were so worn that they looked like oblong slugs. Nothing remained of their lost art and thus of their former value.

The woman's face on one was perfect. So were the sharp arrows with their clearly discernible feathers.

The party ended in this order: the Boy fondled, counted and examined the hoard's coins until he fell asleep, his bottom on the toilet-stool, his top in the sink; The bright poker chips were cashed in and returned to their black bins; All the pennies were counted. Wood Chuck Polansky, with two hundred and thirty seven in his right front pocket, limped through appropriate laughs, like he couldn't walk with such a weight of wealth. The dults finished their drinks; Moose returned to the bathroom, waking up the Boy saying, "Now see, this is the way you do it, you never piss in the puddle, it's too splashy on your shoes, you always pee on the side, that cleans up the stool, unless your aim's bad, oops, that cleans up the floor." More stories were told at the door amid great mirth and positive satisfaction. During the stories the Boy sampled the remains of the drinks, except for the beer. That stank! Finally, the company turned the knob from the outside. Finally-finally, the Boy and his parents put the glasses in the sink to warsh in the mornin'. Searching for any opportunity to make his good day gooder, the Boy asked for permission to sleep on the couch. Super-and-completely, finally, the Boy slept on the couch.

THE PIGEONS

By the time the sleep was washed from the Boy's eyes by his rosy fingers, it dawned on the Boy that it was the middle of the day. It was almost nine o'clock.

His father's saw and hammer had been the alarm-clock-tools that catapulted the Boy from deep sleep to complete alertness.

While the Boy put on his clothes, the bricks of Sanitary Canyon doubled, by echoes, the progress his father was making.

It was because of an impending trip that the Boy's father had hurried so. Well, in part, it was because of the trip. In other parts, it was because he wanted the Boy to have his coop. When he himself was a boy he had enjoyed his pigeons. It was a pleasure that he could enjoy again with his son. He had considered how few of those kinds of joys there were that transcended the changes of both the times and the generations.

The boy within him drew the work from the man. He wanted the puffers, the rollers, and the homers to fly home to his life again. He wanted them to come to the life of his boy.

65

Then, of course, he wanted to finish the coop because he had started it. The Boy's father was Frank Lester. That was cause enough. Frank Lester wanted to finish things! He needed to finish them.

The stories the man told about his youth did come home to the Boy. His father's wishes became the Boy's desires, too. The Boy lived near the pigeons in their rooms at the bridges. He knew it would be fun to try to catch them. It would be fun to learn more about them. He would be the only boy he knew who had pigeons except that other boy, Rudi Thill. The day he would get pigeons was becoming as big as a birthday and the day that school got out. Oozsho! - PIGEONS.

The pigeon coop was half done. The Boy was amazed and pleased.

It stood solidly over its raked foundation... over the closed trenches that had been the home of the hoard. The four corners were 2 by 4s. The roof slanted down from the front to the back. The bottom floor was complete. It was about three feet from the ground. High, the Boy thought...

The thought was interrupted... He was being diverted. He was dancing. He ran to the house. The toilet was calling, shouting, demanding...

His mother intercepted him. She forced the Boy, who couldn't wait to argue, to sit on his old, long abandoned, potty chair. He protested as he acted. He could wait no longer. His butt now barely fit between the arms.

The Boy no longer needed to wonder what his stools were - they were his humiliation.

The Boy's big job completed, his mother joined the list of people who had found the old coin.

The Boy said, "It's too shiny, it's not the same coin." His mother laughed saying, "I guess you soaked it good. During its dark travels it lost its patina somewhere." She speculated that it was a foreign coin, "Probably a French nickel," she said. "If they have nickels."

She could read the words *LIBERTÉ, ÉGALITÉ* and *FRATERNITÉ*. Also *franc*. The date on the coin was 1853. It showed oak leaves and acorns.

The other side featured a woman sowing seeds. It said *RÉPUBLIQUE FRANÇAISE*.

The Boy hollered for his dad to come see the coin but his dad just kept pounding, finishing… The coop was becoming.

Across the back wall of the coop were four decks of nest boxes. Descending vertically from under the roof, on the right, was a wide board with a hole big enough for a pigeon doorway. A little landing board was nailed below that.

The left side sported two boards that the Boy's father was hinging. The vertical one being designed to open when the nests needed cleaning. The horizontal board was for feeding and watering the pigeons.

When the doors were completed a second pigeon entry was made in the front of the coop on the same level as the floor.

The Boy helped his father nail the chicken wire where it was needed.

Oozsho, the coop was ready! Oozsho, the Boy's father was the best-tess arc-a-tick in the world. Oozsho, the best dad too.

Oozsho! the final Oozsho was said hoping that the Old Dam was listening.

THE E-GYP-SEE

While the Boy examined and admired the coop, his father took a bath and shaved. For him it was a rare thing to do in the morning.

The Boy's mother made sandwitches, wrapped them in waxed paper and packed them in her old willow basket.

The Boy fell asleep in the back seat of the old car as it made its way across the beautiful land. He had heard his father repeat his worn adage, "We're going to Dubuque by way of Iowa City." It was appropriate, too, because they had made a wrong turn on the way to the Indian Mounds.

Maybe the Boy had partially heard his mother describing something she had read about a ply-stow-scene flat toe. It was a place where, in the old-olden days, they had icy sheets. He kinda listened to fuzz words, es(carp) ment fish, ice glacier and slumped slump blocks.

As if he, too, had just calved from his parent-rock, he descended the hill into deeper sleep, the stuff of woven dreams gave him a circular basket: the same old willow basket…

His grandfather was saying that the inside of the basket was larger than its outside. Its handles were also feet. Its lid was a hoop.

He didn't need to pay real good attention because it was a family deal that was often told. The basket was a woman. The woman was a mother.

When Nona Ruby was a girl, all of her siblings were not yet born. And yet they were. Twelve was the mother-count. Had she reached a final stage...? Gramma Sills baked this story right into her bread.

A family of Indians, some said E-gyp-sees, some said both, came each summer to camp on the farm along E-gyp-see Creek. That family had twelve kids, too. Not all of them were born yet either.

It was easy for the twenty-eight people to live together in the summer time.

On hot days when only one of the two families bathed in the spring, you could see all twenty-eight of The People united. (Yes, it could have been Uncle Larry speaking.) (He was younger than the Boy who was listening to the story. That was strange.)

(Or, it could have been Aunt Joyce. She could have spoken from deep within the orange glow of her memory mound.)

(But it was Faye who said, "They all could be seen there in the creek, born and unborn, alike." Yes, Uncle Faye said that through the cave of his mouth that flowed through his hollow cheeks.)

...each kid had a companion. Size matched size. Age matched age.

...each kid had a match in athleticis, in spirit and curiostity.

As the Boy slept, his mother read parts from two little books (*A Guide to the Upper Iowa River*, and *Decorah Trails and Trolls*) by George Knudson. "The first white men to set foot on eastern Iowa soil were Joliet and Marquette, who canoed down the Wisconsin River in 1673 to its junction with the Mississippi..." just below the location which later became a French trading post and then the city of Prairie du Chien....

"A celebrated line of Winnebago chiefs have borne the name Decora, probably taken from the name of a French trader, de Carrie, who came to

Wisconsin in 1728 with the French army, resigned his commission three years later to become a fur trader and married a well-known queen of the Winnebagos. Although de Carrie returned to Canada after seven or eight years, his two sons remained with their mother and became chiefs with the name Decora. A grandson of one of these was known as Waukon Decora, and it was this chief who maintained a camp on the Upper Iowa River," between the Whippy Dip and the Sugar Bowl.

One of the matched pairs was Dee Carrie and Nona Ruby. These two spent the summers in and around E-gyp-see Creek. They wore garlands made of Sweet Williams or leis made of a green weed that stuck to itself in the sweetness of late June and early July.

Their special treasure was Jewelweed. They never failed to receive pleasure from its magic. Each with one hand they held it. They melded it into silver when they dipped it into the creek together. Dee Carrie admired it from under water, Nona over. Nona, the ruby, could see solid silver with green veins. Dee was blessed with old-silver droplets under green leaves.

The girls were otters. (It sounded like Aunt Reta's voice telling this part.) They could play forever! Dee was a deep, and Nona a shallow water otter. (Nona loved word combos like that.)

(The voice of the Cliff-born Reta continued)...some of the summer grand fathers received their names from the bluffs along E-gyp-see Creek, upstream near Eagles Nest.

The girls and the boys, the Cliffs intoned, were equals. The sisters were brothers and sisters. The brothers were sisters and brothers, too. The girls were each other, especially when they were on horses. When Dee Carrie and the Ruby, Nona, were on horses they were horses, too.

While riding their drums, they were one. There was not one and the other.

The Boy's Grand Father was a Cliff, too. He could tell the story of "The two girls who were one, yes the families who were one," in ways no other person could.

Because he was a grand father he knew an ending of the unending story of the basket people. Grand mothers knew the story, too.

The story started from a long proud time long ago. That was before all the water in the E-gyp-see ran down stream (the grand parents might have said).

Then Cliff-ford loosened his belt a notch from the twenty-four to the twenty-five inch hole. He took a deep breath. He pushed back his Carl Sandburg hair. He closed his eyes.

"The girls would put their horses through their paces. The hooves rattled the windows in the farmhouse. Their thunder was a heartbeat, half mother-heart, half earth-mother-mother, half father-heart, half father-father-sun. The thunder was our family. All twenty-six of us gathered in the creek, watching, listening, anticipating, not knowing what to expect.

"Dee Carrie's horse was named Crazy. Nona called hers Ruby but it was really Elk.

"Each horse was an appaloosa.

"Dee's horse was white. Nona's horse was black. For the paintings on their rumps they borrowed colors from each other. Nona's horse had some spots that were red surrounded by black. Small sparkles of white made them into rubies. More especially when the spots were wet.

"It was fantastic to see the two, who were one, run through the creek's shallows. Elk ran on the hooves of Crazy, his cousin."

It was at this point in the story that the steep Cliff pulled his chair up to a shiny piece of metal tacked to the floor.

The Boy squirmed. A quirk of ss-kept skept-icism itched him where his belief in Santa Claus tried to live. Even while remaining in the dream, he stepped out of it. Because Doubts itched like a sting weed itch without a jewel juice weed cure.

The Boy watched his grand father lean forward in his chair. He saw him place the balls of his feet on the metal plate. While his toes never left the surface, Cliff pummeled the metal with his heels. A smile fell from the face of the Cliff as he closed his eyes. Then his bony hands began to slap his thighs in rhythm with his feet.

The family watched the hooves of the horses appear and disappear in the reflections of the E-gyp-see Creek. They heard their echoes pounding in the valley floor under the Cliff.

When the girls and their horses were exhausted they stopped in the middle of the stream.

Black Elk dropped his head and deeply sucked in pure water. Crazy Horse reached up his huge lips and with his long teeth chewed a heavy density.

When Nona stretched her tight muscles toward the sky-bright clouds, Dee Carrie reached down into the creek's shadows where she found a simple willow basket hidden in the moss.

The horses pranced and nodded approval when Dee de Carrie offered Nona the willow basket. Its inside Is bigger than its outside. Its lid is a hoop of our nations. The gift is for family from family to family."

Each with one hand they held it. They melded it into silver words with the water.

One silver sentence was black from above, the other silver was white from below. Both of the Jewelweed sentences were otters.

"Mom,-Mom-Mom-an-Dad," the Boy jabbed, "I had the weirdest dream.

"Mom, it was like I was there. In your E-gyp-see Creek stories, but weirder."

The Boy rushed ahead, telling the whole dream. "Your whole family was there! Neil and Dorothy, and Danny and Milton and Lila and Wilma and all the rest. They were all there. Just like real! It was weird, they all had the same letter to start their middle names, R. Weird! RayRuthRalphRubyRowainRossRobertRonninRose Reva Roberta and Roy.

"Richard was there too, at the end of the dream. He explained all about it. He said we all have identical twins when we wade in water.

"He said dreams, like books, are amazing ways to visit the past and the future. He said we could even see ourselves, and sometimes laugh, like tears from the eyes of our reflections."

"Mom, how can we do that? Dad?" He said... he said... he said... "Mom? Dad?"

"Settle down now, you're too excited," Frank said.

"He's right, take it easy," Nona said. "It was an interesting dream. There are things we will never know, from the past and in the future. Mystery is our strangest friend. It plays many games. Now, what was that about my sister Joyce?"

Even though they were a long-a-ways from home, the Boy was chew-er that the Old Dam was listening.

THE CAR-*nivore*

The Boy's family made considerable progress along their way to "Dubuque by way of Iowa City."

They decided to have a pink-a-nink in the car. They ate favey-favorite sand-witches, peanut-butter-and-jelly. Mmmmmmm. Home made wild grape jelly and Peter Pan Peanut Butter. They all liked the taste of the words Peter-Pan-Peanut-Butter, too. They tried to see who could eat those words the fastest. They said some of them too fast, so they didn't count when they were predigested. They had many such games to play when they were riding. The rules were often more fun than the games and led to endless changes.

The basket was now empty, the Boy thought. He had already asked if there were any more sand-witches. Not being satisfied about the answer, he had asked again. And still again because his stomach hadn't remembered that he had asked. A little later he asked once more because he was sometimes a pest when he was cooped up in the car.

The Boy's father responded to this last inquiry quite emphatically! He mentioned that the Boy might get more than sandwiches if he asked again.

The Boy decided that there were no more sand-witches.

Soon after that hard decision, the Boy fell asleep, again. His mother interrupted her oral reading. She checked the back seat to see if the children were OK.

She held up two fingers and smiled at her husband. It was a part of their private sign language. It meant that both kids were sleeping. It also signaled the beginning of a peaceful time of warm contentment and relaxation for the parents. Each of them gave a sigh at the same time. A universal sigh-n language.

When the kids were asleep, Frank was very extra careful not to hit ruts or potholes that would awaken them. He also rolled through stop signs very slowly. He avoided quick braking and any other motoring activities that might disturb the tranquility present in the old black sedan.

As they were leaving McGregor they rounded the corner by the River Rat Cafe. Another car pulled out right in front of them.

The Boy's mother automatically thrust out her left arm to protect her children at the same time Frank hit the brakes.

There was no way to avoid it. They struck the car directly in the bumper and stopped dead.

Nona was shocked to find the Boy beside her. Somehow he had landed in the front seat behind her extended arm.

While Frank was still swearing, both parents investigated to see if the baby was all right.

"The baby," Nona wailed, "where is the baby?"

While his father jumped out of the car, the Boy looked over the seat into the back.

No one was there.

His father couldn't find the baby either.

A wave of panic hacked them.

Not in the car.

Not under the car.

Not in the street.

Not in the ditch.

"Where is he? Where?"

And they heard not even a peep, no cry, no sound of the baby.

The Boy's father even looked in the trunk.

Nothing!

Then he heard a little cooing, like the baby made when he was asleep.

Frank rushed around to the back door. He climbed in and carefully lifted the bottom section of the back seat up and forward toward himself.

There, sound asleep in the seat well, was Steven. Just as if nothing had happened.

The folks from the other car looked in the window. "The seat must have flown up when they hit us," the driver said. She looked as if she understood exactly what had happened.

Everyone examined the cars. They were surprised to find that nothing was broken, "There's not even a leak in the radiator," said Frank.

Slowly, he started the car and drove on, his ear testing the sounds of his motor, hoping to hear its familiar voice. The car cooed like Steven. He was almost relaxed when three miles later they pulled into the parking lot at the Mounds.

THE MOUNDS

Nona didn't go into the museum when the Boy and his father did. She stayed in the car. "I'll wait," she said, "until the baby wakes up." But there was more involved than that. She was a little shaky yet. She was also so very thankful. She needed more time than "the men folk" did, to recover.

When the baby woke up she still didn't want to go into the museum. She carried him up a little path leading to the North Unit Mounds. She was careful not to go so far that she couldn't see the Boy and his father when they came out. She sat down on a little bench overlooking the Yellow River valley.

She was greeted by the whip of a tail and a rather scoldy sounding hello from a chipmunk. It jumped up on the other end of the bench and upon seeing how cozy the baby looked, in his little blanky, it snuggled under its own tail.

The effects of this funny action got a laugh out of Nona. She relaxed and began to feel at home. A rose-breasted grosbeak flew into a small chinquapin oak while singing. Its bright colors said, "Well of course I can sing while I fly, can't you?"

Nona could see that the jack-in-the-pulpits had preached their last sermons. She knew that she would see their resurrection in the fall in the form of clusters of bright red berries.

The may-apples were fruiting. She wanted to try one but she decided that she would wait so that the Boy could taste them with her.

Her senses were still keen; she was sharpening her woodland heritage. She wanted the Boy to share it without the loss of detail.

Then she saw her favorite flower. She whispered to Steven, "It's my 'favey-favorite.'" It was a yellow lady's-slipper.

"Interesting," she said to herself, and maybe to the baby, as she admired its delicacy. "Most of the flowers have human names. I wonder what they think of that?"

"I'll bet," she continued, "that the lady wouldn't be so happy if she knew those bees were in her slippers."

The baby smiled. It was probably gas!

Nona looked down at the cars in the lot, to check. Nope, not yet.

"Mom, Mom," the Boy yelled, "come quick, ya gotta see this. There's a pot in there that's big enough for me to git inside. Come on Mom, hurry. It was broken and someone stuck it back together. It's real neat! There's lots of other good stuff too."

As they climbed the big, long, hill toward the mounds of the South Unit, it became obvious how tired the dults were.

They walked through a darkly shaded area under a canopy of hard maples. The mosquitoes seemed to particularly like this area. Something about the little buzzers revived the speed and energy of the dults.

Then they came to a part of the woods that was primarily oaks. Under the oaks was an understory of prickly-ash and ironwood woods.

Below these they saw a miniature forest of may-apples. To the Boy they looked like umbrellas hiding something. The something, the mother showed the Boy, was their apples. Everyone liked their taste, even Steven, who received one peeled. Most of the family had little prickly-ash scratches when they got back to the path. The Boy had a may-apple berry in each hand. As he walked he alternated taking bites from one hand then the other.

Nona told how the family used to make dolls out of the leaves. "Two or three of the petals of the leaf we pulled down and tied into a skirt. The others we pulled up from the body for arms. We used other flowers for the head. Another may-apple leaf was used as the doll's umbrella. For my favey-faces I used dandy-lions and jack-in-the-pulpits. The one had such a sunny disposition and the other looked like he was enjoying his own singing.

"Oh, look," Nona pointed. "See that thin, dirty, white string? No, over there by that groaty, decayed, morel. That's all that's left of this year's Dutchman's breeches."

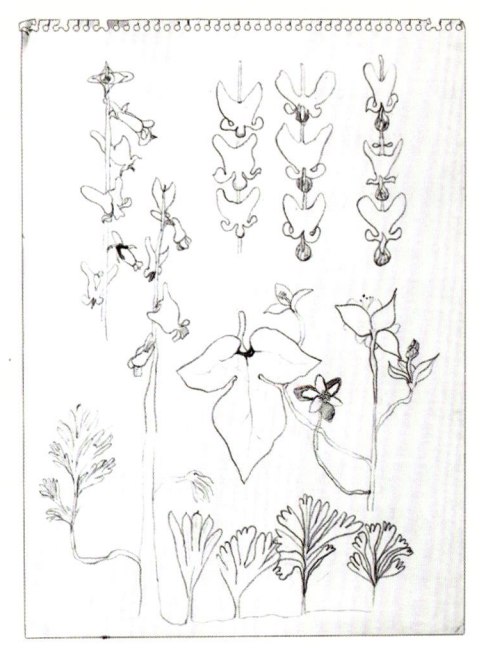

"No, over there by that groaty, decayed, morel. That's all that's left of this year's Dutchman's breeches."

"The Dutchmen sure wore out those pairs of pants," Frank teased.

She, also, teased that way-way back, when she was a little girl, "Boys wore trillium skirts and girls wore Dutchman's stylish britches"

As they walked on, the oaks became poplars, the poplars became sumac, and then the sumac yielded to the sunny prairie.

"Look how tall this grass is," said the Boy.

"Hell to mow," said his dad.

"Not as tall as it's going to get—it's giant-blue-stem, and this is side-oats..." said his mother as the Boy interrupted with...

"It don't look blue to me." But the Boy didn't wait for a response as some unexpected spurt of energy shot him up the trail ahead of the others.

The parents laughed, he looked like a chipmunk. The baby laughed, too, because his parents were laughing.

About two city-blocks ahead (the Boy always measured in city blocks) the Boy froze. Exactly as he did in his playground game Freeze.

His eyes were bigger and older than his body.

There, ahead of him, stood a herd of deer, their heads sticking out of the tall grass. Their ears were alert, bodies' tense, white tails standing straight up. Neither the Boy nor the deer moved.

Because the Boy didn't move, the deer couldn't see him.

His attention was drawn automatically to the biggest buck. The Boy could see every detail. Even the nervous twitch in its shoulder.

He could see the brown of its giant eye. Nothing moved except for that twitch and the eye's thoroughy g-l-o-b-u-l-a-r, in-vesss—tigation...

The buck must have been receiving at least two messages. The odor of the Boy was one.

Then the Boy saw a thirteen-stripped ground squirrel in the open path, right below the deer.

The little fellow gave the buck his other eye.

With legs, tail and sassy mouth, all acting as one, the ground squirrel suddenly jumped, whipped its tail and sharply scolded.

The big buck, as if his feet were tied together, sprang high up and landed four feet behind where he had stood.

Too late, in mid-air he recognized his foolish error.

His eye, however, was not the same eye when he landed. It was now two embarrassed eyes, each receiving the inquiring glances of the does.

Then the eye made another change.

The buck jumped backwards again, exactly as he had before but with added showmanship. He did it one more time as if he always did that before prancing.

Then head held high, chin tucked, he arched his right foot smartly at the ankle. He followed this by a precise jerk upward at the knee. Then at exactly the same interval, he majestically lifted his leg even higher from the shoulder. Each leg, alternately, followed the first to join into his royal prance. The buck dipped his horns to the squirrel, who was paying the same amount of attention as were the does.

The Boy laughed.

All the deer, as if they were one, bounded across the grass and leaped into the sumac. Then they ran into the woods waving their white flags good-bye, good-bye…

"Dad, Dad, come quick," the Boy yelled. "Ya gotta see this."

Of course, when the family got there, both the ground squirrel and the deer were gone.

"Sure," Frank kidded after the Boy blurted out the story. "Sure... sure you saw that. Yaa... Yap, I suppose so. He must be that big bad buck who's the ham in Bucking-ham Palace. Right?"

Even though they were a long-a-ways from home, the Boy was chew-er that the Old Dam was listening.

THE SYMPHONY

P - s - s - s - s - s - s - s - s

The Boy ran ahead, again. About four city blocks later, he saw a little trail lead off to the left into prickly ash and ironwood trees. That looks like a deer path, he thought, and these trees are more my size.

It suddenly opened into what looked to him like a golf course. There was a long narrow fairway that was well mowed. But, it would be difficult to play golf there because wherever the golf ball might land, it was sure to roll off into the woods. A long ridge ran down its center. It's almost a city block long, the Boy thought.

80

Then the Boy was surprised by another thought. The golf course was like a cemetery. He wasn't sure how. Its peacefulness was a little spooky.

He turned and walked back through the little opening in the woods where he had entered the eerie place. He would feel better if he were with his parents. (Although he would never say so.)

"Mom-Mom-Mom-an-Dad," he recited his pome, "Ya gotta see this."

The little family now ducked and wound their way through a green tunnel before entering the opening together. Not with the same burst of energy that the Boy had before, but with respect.

Frank pointed out that Indians had made the mound a thousand years ago. This one was called a linear mound. They had seen pictures of these in the museum.

Nona extended a hand, which asked for silence. They heard a blue jay singing - oliver, oliver, oliver. She whispered, "They only sing that song on perfect days." There were a dozen other jays singing, too. Mixed with olivers they could hear metallic chimes, bronze songs from silver throats. She identified those as blue jays, too.

As they walked on through this immersion in blue songs, a red and a copper cardinal dipped across the opening ahead of them. Soon a jay-jay-jay-warning alerted all the crested blues to fly deeper into the shade. From that sanctuary they raucously began speaking still another language.

The family sat on the mound. Nona spread the baby's blanket and Frank laid him down on his back. Relieved from the burden of carrying, Frank shook his arms. His shoulders relaxed.

The Boy looked toward the basket.

Nona said, before the Boy could even open his mouth, "No, there are no more sand-witches."

She still wanted to talk blue jays. She said that the ones they had seen represented at least three generations. "The old folks and the yearlings are working together to bring up this year's young. They're very intelligent," she continued, "they even use tools."

"I wonder how many songs the smartest bird can sing?" Nona wondered. "Try to count the ones you hear. See how many you can learn!"

In these woods there are singers singing in Oneota dawns: in skies of Zuni-turquoise; in Sauk sparkling daylight diamonds; in Ho Chunks of sunset and Apache-tear-drops of night.

The Boy heard birds singing in ways he never had before. Their individual calls gathered themselves into a single song like the orchestra the Boy had

The birds singing in the woods
The woods singing in the birds

heard at the Paramount Theater. Each bird sounded like an instrument. The overall effect was complex like that. But there in the woods the birds were composing and singing and playing. They were doing everything at the same time.

Nona, the Ruby, asked the Boy if he could hear any birds that sounded like musical instruments.

Put put put put put put put put put put.

"That one sounds like a drum," he said.

"It's a ruffed grouse," his mother taught.

"Or someone starting an old John Deere tractor," laughed his father.

"Do those sound like horns?" the Boy asked. "I think they're turtledoves."

"Yes they do sound a little like English horns, and yes, they are doves. Good for you!"

"I can hear wrens too, just like the ones that live in the houses nailed to the lumber yard by the dam. But I can't figure out any instruments?"

"They sound like piccolos to me," she said.

"Are those the little flutes?"

"Yes."

"They're just my size, I like those."

"They're energetic like you, too."

"That one, wow, that one's exciting, and scary, there he is, right up there. He sounds like air coming out of a tire."

    P - s - s - s - s - s - s - s - s - s

"You're right, and he could think that he's a scree-chee violin too, but he's really a red-tailed hawk," said Frank. "When he's hungry for his supper he sometimes eats the birds who are the instruments in his orchestra.

"When he gangs up with other violins, for a concert though, they usually only try to scare the voices out of the other instruments."

    P - s - s - s - s - s - s - s - s

"That sure quieted down the woods," said the Boy.

"Yes it did, but I can still hear the flutes that the hermit thrushes are playing, so mysteriously, way back in the woods. How they can sound like a magic toast struck with crystal glasses, gongs, chimes, and flutes at the same time, I'll never know," Nona quietly added.

"That's a pheasant, in an open field," Frank said. He's playing the rusty gate. Blue jays can play that old squeaky gate, too."

"Rib-it," the Boy said, ribbing his father, "I know the frog-bird song, rib-it, rib-it!"

They all laughed, the baby, too, because they were laughing.

A quiet pause settled on the family. The listening had become a kind of game. The birds cooperated by continuing their concert. The Boy received the gift.

Their interest was again roused when they heard a barred owl, the conductor of the woods, ask

"Who who - who-hoo?   Who who - Who-hoo?" (me?")

to the tuxedoed crows in a nearby tree. Apparently the crows had not been paid for their last concert. It was quite a rookus-ruckus. CAWCAWCAW CAW Aw-er...rrr.err-rook...We were rooked...It's rrrob-berrry! Rr-report this err-rook-by hook orrr crook of our roock- rockery to the ee-union the musicians union.

The whole family, even Steven, (it could have been gas) was laughing. The crows and the owl were so mad at each other that they didn't pay any attention to anything else.

The Boy began to experiment with the songs around him. He was becoming a bird. A bird and the woods. He wanted to make music.

It worked in his head. He heard the birds within him there. But his efforts to whistle their song got lost on his tongue near his lips. He couldn't quite figure it out. He decided that even though it was hard for him to do, it would be worth learning how to do it. He'd practice.

His mother broke into his thoughts as if she could read part of his mind. "Antonin Dvorak listened to the birds, up in Spillville.

"He may have had a hard time with his English, but he sure could understand the songs of the birds. After he wrote down their musical notes on paper, an eye could tell an ear how it sounded. His magic music made birds in his recreation of their New World Symphony."

       Peep
  Ch*eer*-up   c*heer*-up
Zin*k*   Zin*k*   Zin*k*

Aw Aw-aw Aw Aw-aw….AW-*er..rrr.err*-Rook… CAW CAW CAW
Nit nit nit Nit nit Nit nit nit Nit

  Coo – oo *oo*   *ooo*   *o*
  Coo – oo *oo*   ooo   *Ooo oo oo*

Oliver   *Oliver*   *Oliver*
      Nit Nit

Pee-EE *Wee*   Pee-EE *Wee*   Pee-ee *Wee*

Put put oo put oo   put put put put – put – put put.

Chipchip-chip Jay cheer-up ooo oo – Caw oo Jay iver-iver
    Jay *P* ee *w*ee-wepeely, wepeelee
    Aw s – s – s – s – s – s

Nona said, "This is what will fill the woods tonight!"

Whip-or-will Whip-or-will Whip-poor-Will Whip-or-will Whip-poor-will
Whip-or-will Whip-or will Whip-poor Will Whip-or-will Whip-poor-will
    Don't whip poor-Will-Whip

Who Who *Who*-hoooAWK Who Who *WHo*-hooAWK *Whip*-Who-*O*r-will
Who-*Whip*
   Zin*K* Zin*K* Zin*K* EEE Eee EEE ee *E*
Szzzzzzzzzzzzzzzzzzzzzzzzzzzzzzzzzzzzzzzzzzzzzzzzzzzzzzz*inK*
RibitRibitRibit RibitRibit Rib Ribit-
    Put-put.

    COCK-A-DOODLE DO
    ~~~~~~~~~~~~~~~

THE BEARS

The enchantment with the birds was diverted because the baby turned over on his stomach for the first time. This action put Steven into the center of attention. He did it again, as if to say, I could always do that.

That's an awkward movement, the Boy thought. It required that the baby extend his right arm. Then, as if it were going to look back at the basket, the head's weight rolled the whole body over.

Look at that little neck, the Boy gawked, it can't even lift its own head.

Frank and Nona made quite a to-do about it. The Boy considered doing a summersault to retrieve the center of attention. He would have, last year, but now he was trapped in an uncomfortably new age of awareness.

Instead, while his parents rolled Steven over to his back again, in hopes of a third showing, the Boy reached his dirty thumb up to his mouth. It was gooood, for as long as it lasted, but it didn't last long! A searchlight of scrutiny was always at-the-ready to shine on him when he was enjoying his thumb. This time, his mouth was interrogated before his thumb was placed under arrest.

The baby began to cry because he thought the scolding was for him.

The parents saw their error, too late, and settled for feeling bad. "It's unanimous," said Frank, after Nona picked up the baby.

Steven stopped crying by the time Frank brushed the grass off the blanket and folded it. The family drug themselves along the path in a raveled little knot.

They saw several conical mounds through the tree trunks up ahead. The "men folk" perked up by repeating what they had learned about them in their museum visit. They had studied a drawing of the positions of the mounds. They walked directly toward the first bird effigy as if they were walking in their own yard. "It's a zinker mound," the Boy smiled.

From the woods on their left someone started another John Deere tractor. "No Frank," Nona corrected Frank's humor, even before he had expressed it, "It's a ruffed grouse." As they neared the big bird mound, more tractors started…

Put put put put put put put put put put.
Put put put put put put put put put put.
Put put put put put put put put put put.

From the center of the mound they seemed to hear it clearest. Indeed, a strange heartbeat was beating, beating!

The Boy looked at the basket.

His mother saw him and shook no again, there were still no sand-witches in the basket-basket, the basket.

But, this time, that wasn't what the Boy was thinking.

The family knot was still tied as they all walked toward the next mound.

It was a bear.

The information in the museum had identified this mound as one of the "marching" bears. On the hillside ahead of them stretched an impressive string of these bears, lying on their sides, in the mowed dogleg. "'Marching' bears?" thought the Boy's father. "How could these be 'marching' bears? They look so peaceful. They're not arranged in an exact line like a column of militaristic bears. Yes, they're meandering bears! No, ambling bears. Ya!

"Ambling bears? Yes!" That was the end of Frank's conjecture. He had completely decided that they were not Marching Bears. They were ambling, playful bears! Perhaps, they were a family of bears tumbling on a green blanket.

Nona spread the blanket on the bear and they all sat down.. This time she took out ten bear claws from the basket. She carefully arranged them into a necklace in the center of the blanket.

Suddenly the Boy heard a screech that pierced his ears.

"Ooozsho", the Boy Ooozshoed, three red-tails!

P - s - s - s - s - s - s - s - s - s

The boy answered,
"P - s - s - s - s - s - s — s"

"P - s - s - s - s - s,"
said Nona.

The Boy looked at the basket again. "Sand-witches?" he thought; "No," he knew better than that, "But what else was in the basket?"

His mother said, "Chew-er, go ahead, look."

This time it was empty.

When the Boy's family stood beside the bear, they could see that it was the last of the amblers. Beyond the bear there were two zinker-bird mounds sculpted as if they were ready to fly out over the Mississippi.

The Boy was imagining how wonderful it would be to hear the shuttering sounds these enormous birds might make when they pulled out of a dive.

The Boy enjoyed what his parents said about the mounds and the Mississippi below them.

His mind had traveled to a time all his own. He was very good at that. He flew far out over the river like an eagle.

Miss Darling would like what he said about that. Leo would be jealous.

Dusk was getting heavy when they got back to the car. Frank took a potato-fork out of the trunk. The "men folk" dug wild parsnip in the ditch. Nona carefully placed it in the basket.

Nona, again, warned the Boy about the dangers of touching the leaves when they are wet. Or, when he was wet. He already knew all about that. He had the scars to prove it. The wild parsnips had known exactly how to teach him.

The Boy was even hungrier now. He imagined the goodness of the sweet roots. He remembered, out loud, that they tasted like carrots.

"They're better because they're wild and they're free," his father added.

It was very unusual for the little family to eat out. But much-to-the-Boy's surprise, they stopped at the River Rat Cafe, for a late supper.

The Boy tried one of their famous "mushroon ham-mur-mers."

Nona had a salad with dressing on the side and fresh catfish.

Frank teased the waitress, "Don't put any of those damned 'mushroons' on my 'ham-mur-mer."

They split two orders of French fries. Mmmmmmmm.

Steven liked those, too, soaked with some milk from his bottle.

The Boy liked milk too, so he dunked his ham-mur-mer.

Almost as soon as the four were in the car, Nona held up two fingers. Soon after that Frank could have held up three.

He had to fight off four. However, the fresh memory of the accident prevented him from falling into the sleep his body craved.

The Boy dreamed that he was playing basketball. Shirley Myers stood in the center jump circle. She wore a cheerleader sweater that said FILLMORE. It hung on her just like the FILLMORE jersey hung on the Boy. Since she was the purest, she was chosen to throw the ball up, to start the game.

The Boy stood at the outside edge of the circle. Wild parsnips sores festered under his uniform. They distracted him. Even with all the fans watching, his fingers scratched and scratched.

Carp, catfish and crappie fans watched from the grandstand at the Old Dam.

An unreticulated quillback carpsucker, the referee, put his whistle to his mouth. He blew, blew furiously, but only bubbles came out. The Old Dam couldn't hear those, even if he was listening.

THE SANDMAN

The early morning summer sun was early. He was one of the Boy's fathers. He leaped through the window into the Boy's familiar bedroom to warm the Boy's day. He did his routine floor exercises as he walked across the Boy's linoleum floor. That usually woke the Boy. But even after the floor was warm, the Boy was still sleeping.

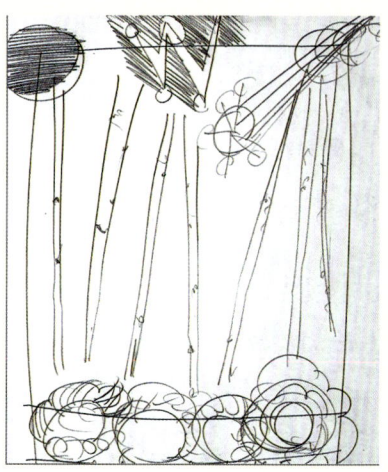

The sun climbed up the wrinkled sheet and over the edge of the bed. He paused at the top, and then he pounced on the place where he often initiated his wrestling matches with the Boy. Instead, he landed on a mound of sloth, bed-sloth.

Slowed by the surprising shock of the Boy's default, the sun snailed back into his circular shell of clouds mumbling to himself, "Well I can't win them all. I guess the Sand Man pinned the Boy in the first period of his match last night."

By the time the sun's cloud of disappointment dissipated it was time for him to spring into another boy's room in Omaha, then Denver, then… There are literally millions of boys that Father Sun wrestles with each morning. And, an almost… equal number of boys who are eager to tussle with their Father during the creation of his wonderful, one-of-a-kind mornings: each and every single awesome one after another.

Where the sun had failed, the vulgar alarm clock succeeded. It disguised itself in the form of the Referee's whistle during the ball game that the Boy had continued to play all night long. The little ball in the ref's whistle that jumped up and down screaming FOUL ended his dreams!

Frank had been so tired the night before that he had set the alarm out of habit, forgetting the welcome "lazy fair" attitude of his own vacation.

The Boy discovered himself in his own bed. The second sound he heard was Oliver, Oliver, Oliver. It was a beauty-full day. The Boy's eyes had been zipped shut with sleep one minute and were unlashed, were wide awake, the next.

He exploded from bed.

He became a projectile

That landed on his parents' bed.

He said, almost shouting.

"I'm ready to catch pigeons."

He got no response.

He looked at the closed eyelids of the dults. He could see that the sleep in his parents' eyes was not just zippers, it was mucilage, it was eye glue, glued tight.

The Boy sat, waiting, wiggling.

"I'm ready to catch pigeons," he mumbled, but still got no answer. "Impossible," he might have thought.

But the man who was as ancient as sand, the Sand Man, was happy. "These parents are certainly responsive to my magic," he thought as he looked in upon Frank and Nona. He was a credit to their happiness. That was obvious. And. And, he had done a pretty good job on the Boy, too. After all, he had succeeded where even Sun Man had failed. "Rare—rare, with a boy like that," the Sand Man said to himself.

He began to busily reorder extra sleep for Saturday night. Saturday nights were great. They were so rewarding because of his hard work and because of the nature of Sunday mornings. He, himself, slept Sunday nights. He deserved it! Besides, there was not much he could do about Monday mornings. The Industrial Revolution had killed Monday mornings. Killed every possibility for a Monday morning snoooo-zer. Monday mornings were kaput!

Vacations were the best part of his year. Everyone praised him during vacations, "Except those darn kids, that is." Vacations were like the whole year used to be when the Sand Man was a kid.

He was working on a new form of sleep. A real eye-clogger, one that would last longer, one that would require less sand and more cement. He would reverse the theory used in connection with pills: smaller doses for kids. He would use a triple portion of cement just for keeping kids' eyes shut on vacation mornings. Maybe a quadruple dose for Saturday vacation mornings. He would recommend a penalty if they still woke up too early. He would prescribe an entire bottle of Cod Liver Oil, one drip at a time, "By golly. Darn kids."

"Every job seemed to have some problems," he thought.

The Sand Man didn't like change. He was a sand-bagger when it came to change.

Why, he could remember when there was no such thing as work. Then that darned Industrial Revolution came along. That was the most revolting revolt! That was the end of good-old-fashioned, daily catnaps, the kind people used to take every day, all during the day, and still be able to sleep at night, too.

Cats are smarter than people now. "Did you ever see a cat with an alarm clock," he thought.

"Or did you ever see a cat jump right out of bed and rush off to work, without even stretching? Work?"

"The Sand Cat. Now there's a cool cat," said the Sand Man, right out loud. The Sand Cat never needs to go to work. A good cat, even a bad cat, will lie down, turn on its gentle motor and ffffffta, just like that, his eyes are filled, just like that. With no help at all.

"Oh yes, those were the good old days. In the good old days people were cats too.

"Before vacations were instigated as an incentive to boost production, a cruelty invented by the revolution, every day was a vacation. Kids didn't cause any trouble then because everyone was a kid. That was before the words Boss and Dult and Laborer were fabricated: quarried, smelted, molded or forged into words of servitude," he continued to think.

"Clocks, factories, schools, overtime, homework, weekdays; hell, they were all contrived at the same time.

"Life used to be good for a Sand Man."

(Even the word Sand Man disappeared if one ventured back farther than the In-Dust-Real Evolution.)

The Sand Man decided that he "…should file a petition to have his job description changed to the Eye-Goo-Guru, or Sleep Man Sleep, or the Eyelash Zipper, or maybe the Mucilage Kid. Yes, and, Snooz-er-oo, man that had a certain ring to it. (Many years later he invented Velcro.)

He pondered the thought that it would be a good idea to leave a pencil and paper on each pillow so people could write down suggestions as soon as they woke up. "Perhaps some of the suggestions might lead to a creative, accurate, or maybe, even a sleep inducing job description."

Oh, how the Sand Man's mind wandered.

"…But, I must get back to work," he grimaced. He was ordering a whole truckload of the little bottles of glue he currently favored. They were the same kind that children used in school. The bottles looked like little ducks. They had a rubber head with a slit on top. The head was flexible. When the Sand Man pushed the head gently down over a sleeper's eyes, the goo-glue ooozed so wonderfully out.

He appreciated the high quality engineering that assisted him when he smeared the glue around the whole eye to effect a longer than usual night of sleep. (He ignored the fact that the rev-a-evolution produced the engineers who engineered the goo guu. He was a situation ethicistic pragmatist-tist.)

Sometimes he spent a little extra time with his favorites, the kids who never wanted to get up no matter what time a day it was. At those times he glued an extra margin of goodness, of sleep, in an attempt to reproduce the natural sleep from the good old times he lived when he was younger, when people were still hunters and gatherers. "That was a good time, yes it was!

"Yes, that was a good time," the ancient Sand Man thought, forgetting he had just been thinking that. "A time before clocks, before time clocks." (It's no wonder some people sleep longer than others, that old Sand Man being so forgetful, and all. Sometimes, he might have glued and glued as he wished and wished.)

"The days of the hunters and the gatherers, the preclock period, those were the good old times," the lugubrious glue man lugubriated.

It was a long wait for the Boy. (Any wait was long for a boy who itched to catch pigeons.) The Boy just couldn't accomplish anything with his parents. They were hopeless!

He shook the bed.

He waited another long minute.

He shook the bed twice.

Frank pulled the cover of warm straw up so only his nose stuck out. He mumbled from his deep den. He was the Bear in the Beaver Park Zoo.

Nona, the slumbering ruby, contentedly cooed like the pigeons the Boy wanted to catch.

He waited another excruciating second.

Impossible!

He shook the bed SEVERAL times.

He waited, erect, a hawk over two squabs.

All he could hear was an even deeper breathing from the opossum.

The Boy spoke again.

The bear and the opossum pulled their noses deeper into the den and seemed to put steel bars between themselves and the Boy. The cooing continued reminding the Boy of the squabs he wanted to catch. It looked like they were snuggling closer under there. "Gad - Zooo!" What an impossible zooo those parents were.

It was dis-cuss-sting!

All the Boy could conjure was a hump of hibernation.

It was dis-cuss-sting!

Sooo, the Boy converted himself into a red-tailed hawk that whistled a bewildered whistle

   P s s s s s s s s

as he leapt into the air and flew from the bed.

He landed as a coyote-ee, who slammed the bedroom door.

As a white-tailed buck, he pranced into the bathroom, but as a Moose, he left the bathroom door open.

Then as a boy paying no respect for the previous directions of a parent Moose, he peed right into the middle of the stool's puddle. That made a LOUDER noise. Noise WAS wanted.

A barely discernible smile curled the corners of the Fox's mouth as he recalled the Moose saying, "Piss on it little man." But he wasn't a little man now, he was turning into a horse.

"Boy," the Horse said to himself, pre-intending, "I chew-er can piss LOUD." (And he could, too!) "We Horses, chew-er can save up, and we gotst bladders that can rilly hold it, and fire-hose it, just like this, just like we do for parades on the First Avenue Bridge."

He giggled and jiggled the jiggler as loud as he could as he flushed. He flushed the flusher twice.

He bolted. He stomped across the kitchen in a herd, among all the animals that he was. They all tromped, together, across the hollow drum that was the back porch. He looked at the sky and immediately became a blue jay.

Oliver?   ("God, what a day.

Oliver,   It sings

Oliver.   With a skip and a swing.")

"Oliver!" said the boy jay, "YES, it's a real OLIVER!"

But, upon a closer investigation, the blue wasn't quite right in the sky. And the Boy's shoulders were slump-ed, just a little. And try as he might, the Boy still could not conjure interest in an empty pigeon coop. It was emity-emity-emityyy. Could there be a false Oliver?

Impossible!?.,~ * +

Leo was nowhere to be found. Ronnie was prolly reading...

BREAKFAST!

Breckfust, the Stomach thought. Breckfust. Yes, the Boy thought, it is time to be a Stomach.

"Stomachs always get attention. They're hungry for attention."

The Boy finished his Wheaties, "Breakfast of Chump Yons." He read the box. The Boy wondered if Ronnie also read the nickel, dime and one box top solicitations of Mr. Wheaties. Or if Leo read the latest about their hero, Jim Thorpe, on the side panel.

The Stomach poured a third bowl of the producers of Chump Yummms. The Boy turned the box to read the other side while he added milk. "They" spilled the milk because "they" were trying to do a different thing at the same time together.

could be reached by descending a choice of several stair steps. One headed downstream, perhaps for a pink-a-nink. Another descended upstream, maybe for a riverside walk. People often skipped rocks, fished, sunbathed or kissed in this catwalk retreat.

The Boy abandoned the area whenever he stumbled upon any discust-sting kiss-sing. But, at the same time, he peeled at least one keen eye and one peeled ear so he could repeat every detail to Young Ronnie. Ronnie was very interested in architecture.

On top of the cement wall was a cement fence that framed a river view of the Coliseum. The catwalk was topped with a sculpted railing perched on short fat columns. The Boy had been dared to walk on the top slab more than once. His fears never yielded to requests to demonstrate bravery, or foolishness. He could remember a little girl he had seen sitting on the railing watching a parade. She could have become a Humpty Dumpty, in front of all the king's horses and all the king's men. But she didn't fall; a king's sandman saved her as she began to fall into the River.

Much to the Boy's chagrin, instead of going directly to the bridge to catch the squabs, Frank walked by the First Avenue Bridge and continued down the river walk to where Van Cleeves' barbershop was located. It was the Boy's favey-favorite barbershop. It had big windows that overlooked the river and May's Island. But, all that didn't matter. The Boy wanted to catch squabs! It was taking hours for his father to wait for his turn. It was taking the Boy weeks, months, years, and he didn't even need an old haircut. The Boy watched the people walk and the river flow. When he looked across the river he forgot being mad because he fell into one of his own rooms.

The Boy's island is called May's Island. It's the Île de la Cité of the Cedar rapids.***** (The stars are derived from the rating system in the Miss Chelin Green Guide to Cedar Rapids, English and Czech edition.) (If the Boy had written a guide, everything would have been measured in comparison to The Old Dam.) There are just about enough stars in Old Glory to live up to the amount of real stars he thought the Old Dam deserved. In his book he could just show the flag of many stars after the name The Old Dam. That would be sufficient to suffice.

The head of the island was cemented into a small park, cement seat encircled. If you stood in this windy little First Avenue prow, you could see the most Beauty-full bridge in town. It was so spectacular that it was given two names: The F Avenue Bridge***** and the B Avenue Bridge, (depending on what side of town you were from) and the ankles of the Old Dam, upstream. And…and… that view***** of the Boy's living room was better than a Queen's view of Louis' Versailles.

Looking behind, you could see the façade of The Coliseum, the Veterans Memorial Coliseum.*****

Your eyes would now be involved in the Boy's history of western architecture.

What you couldn't see was Grant Wood's big stained glass window***** in the rear-facade on Second Avenue.

The Boy could hear his parents starting to move around in the bedroom. They emerged from the last paragraph of the Wheaties box accompanied by long, arm-stretching yawns.

The opossum said, "I get the bathroom first."

The Bear shuffled over and plunked down on a tubular steel chair that bob bob bobbed Frank a good mornin.

The sleep was still so heavy around The Bear's eyes that his head slumped. His hand, independent, seemed to be searching for something usually present on the table.

"Nonnna" the Bear bellowed, "when you're done in there can you make me some coffee? And hurry, will you? I gotta go, too."

This was a dad the Boy had seldom seen. Frank was up and usually gone to work when the Boy awakened.

The Boy monkneed-around while his parents ate their breakfast. He fidgeted, he monkneed, he fidgeted, he monkneed some more. Even as a boy, he was, in small part, an old man.

When his parents were done eating, the Bear put his hand on his Cub's head and roughed-up his hide.

"Let's go" the Bear roared, as he swatted the Cub on the butt. "But, first, warsh your face and brush your chompers."

The Boy kept interrupting his brushing and his warshing by scratching himself through his pants and underpants. This he accompanied with a squirming shuffle-step that was not his "I have to pee" dance.

An itching seemed to have decided to worry him where his undershorts were tight. Under the bands around his legs seemed worst. Below the elastic stomach band, it irritated all the way around.

A choreographer was at work.

Finally, they were ready to go.

THE COLISEUM

The Boy wanted to carry the orange crate with its rope and gunnysack. It was big, and he hoped that it looked heavy to those who might see him struggling toward the bridge. Frank carried a small roll of chicken wire. The contrast of the men folk and their loads was amusing.

The Boy's living room, that included the First Avenue Bridge that they walked toward, was a class of its own, class-iculy Beauty-full to the Boy.

Many aspects of the room were built remembering the French occupation of the city. The artistic fingers of the Parisian Seine touched every aspect.

The Boy's room is a cement Paris, an improved plaster of Pear-ee. Cement! Cement is Wonder-full. Cement formed some of the floor, most of the walls, sometimes even the ceilings of the Boy's rooms. Cement is a crème de la crème hardened into the strength of the Old Dam and his brothers, the other walls of the Boy's room. Cement is the statue of liberty given by The People, of the Empire of Rome, to The People, of The Cedar's rapids. It is the ancient sister of the Statue of Liberty given to The People, of America, by The People, of France.

Some sides of the Boy's river room were palisades of Carrara marble cement. At the base of the western escarpment, was a riverine-catwalk that

What you might hear, if you were standing near the prow's man-hole-cover, were the sounds of traffic or the squabs in their nest in the flying arches, not sooo-far below. The Boy became even more itchy when his imagination heard the squabs.

One of the things that the Boy saw when he looked at the top of the Coliseum from his favey-favorite prow was what he saw on the tail of a nickel, a bit of Monticello.

If the Boy only had a penny, and he held it, tail end up, in front of the Coliseum, he could see two images of the Lincoln Memorial. And from that Memorial he might have been able to see the Parthenon in Athens, that is, if he continued the use of his imagination, or if he traded his Lincoln for a Greek penny.

But with no money at all, which was almost always the case, the Boy could still admire the Tomb of the Unknown Soldier. He saw it through the warm haze of The Teaching of the Pallus-Miss Darling about the Palladium of Cedar Rapids and his own loosely-sketchy choosy learning. So, forget what dults might see and say and try to think boy: No Lincoln sits in this Lincoln Memorial, like he does in Warshington, D.C. so, the col-umes are Lincoln's ribs. His head is the top of the building rising above the cage of his ribs.

"We should be thankful to remember and remember to be thankful, forever and ever. Amen." The rosy finger of Miss Darling's tongue said something like that.

"And the cargo in the May's Island ship is heavily laden with memory, sacrifice, and the reflections of our culture's architectural past. With this precious essence in its HOLD, our future is moving upstream."

"Come into my room," the Boy may have added.

Beaux Arts was the name some Art historians applied to the Boy's Coliseum.

"Bowe-zar," he might have been encouraged to pronounce. But prolly not. "Bowes Arts," most likely, if it came up at all. But the Boy loved, his colossus, his Coliseum, during a wonderful period when the values of life were available, and accepted, just for the liking. It was a simple and direct period, for the Boy.

The building was the most Beauty-full building in the world. Period!

So, relieved of certain responsibilities by simplicity, the style of architecture became known as Boy's Arts. That pronunciation is likely to remain sooo.

Great appreciations grow from early values. There are lotss of wayss to say aesstheticss. Boy's Arts, yes that seems final, the building was the most Wonder-full building in the world.

Mr. Beaux was also partly responsible for the Court House and the Post Office and Quaker Oats and the Merchants Enter-national Bank, the Hotel Roosevelt hotel and the Frank Right People Bank.

What Grant Wood's Sainte Chapelle***** window saw from the Second Avenue facade of the Coliseum, was a grassy park* that was a city block long. The Boy could see it clearly from the barber's window. That was where Leo sometimes went, on Saturday mornings, to learn more about marbles. Framed by the park was Leo's stately Courthouse.***

What Wood's window couldn't see was Notre Dame de Paris,***** that beautiful crown of the Île de France.***** Years later, when the Boy would see that great monument of art history, he still would not see a building more Beauty-fuller than the crown of Cedar Rapids, the Coliseum in his own living room.

Located behind the Courthouse, across the tracks(-)*** of the CRANDIC (the world's first acronym - The Cedar Rapids and Iowa City) Railroad, was the common jail.(-)** Every afternoon ducks accumulated, behind the jail, on the sandy tail of the island, for corn.

All in all, it was a delight-full G-god and man made island, a splendid living room.

Finally, the haircut was finished.

THE BRIDGE

As the Boy and his father arrived under the First Avenue Bridge, the pigeons exploded from their home inside it. The wing claps, joined by the echoes of those claps, scared the bee-jeebers out of the Boy. His hands, which had already started to tickle with excitement, now shook. He put the orange-crate on the rocks under the bridge. A small amount of water formed a slow current next to the first pier.

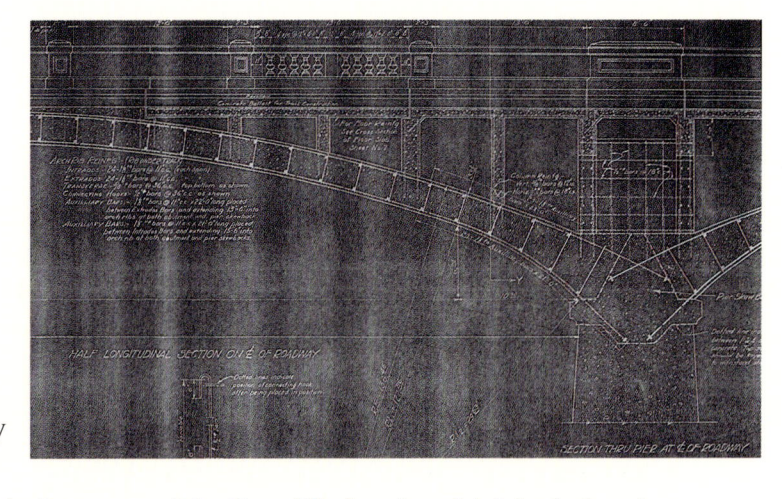

Frank said, "The water's rilly low," as he tossed the chicken wire on the crate.

The Boy put his foot in a stirrup of his father's hands. He shinnied up his dad's ribs and grunted onto his shoulders. He put one foot up on his father's baseball hat. Then very wobbily, the other foot reached the top of the head, too.

Frank grasped both of the Boy's ankles and told him to stiffen his legs and his back and to keep leaning into the wall.

The Old Dam watched as Frank's fingers boosted their boy up until his reaching hands were over the ledge. Then, when the Boy was inside the bridge, the Old Dam smiled because he could hear a monknee, breathing inside his Uncle Bridge.

The first word that might have been heard by the Boy himself was the word that he had just uttered, ooz-sho? It was asked so quietly that only the squabs and the cement and perhaps the Old Dam could hear. His father did not hear it. It was a word that was not uttered as a question in his old world. It was answered by a series of questions in the form of echoes off unseen concrete walls in another new world. This room had once been new to fathers, uncles, and grandfathers when they were young. It is storied that Uncle Gail prolly played his harmonica here.

103

It is a hand-me-down and a boost-me-up roost for many-many boys from Cedar Rapids, a room where family stories have grown for generations, where stories are growing now.

The First Avenue Bridge is a hotel of rooms. The room the Boy stood in was the first room in an avenue of abridging rooms. Closets, toilets, dens, attics, cages, galleries and treasure chests... It is a room full of diaphanous history.

But, what first surprised the Boy was that what he saw was cement, sterile cement. Concrete. Otherwise, there was zip-zero, zipp-o, naught, unless you count the darkness… and the mystery, and the fear. The room was filled with a large population of those guys. Yet, it was understandable that even when his eyes were adjusted and when he saw no squabs, he could already begin to feel the details of the old stories. He heard the peeps and breathed the stink of squab shit. But, where are the babes?

He observed that five of the six sides of the room were closed. He understood that the darkness was caused by the fact that the room opened into the middle of the bridge's underbelly. The back wall of the room was the end of a cave, the reverse side of the bridge's facade. Had this wall been open, the sun could have entered to make it into an entirely different world.

The Boy stood crooked because the trench formed by the arching floor and the vertical wall compressed his left foot. His right foot was several inches higher because of the arch's arch. Even when he realized that he was standing funny, he continued to do so, because his discoveries kept bombarding him faster than he could process them.

The room was more like a closet, he thought, like a long thin closet under the eaves of his Grand Father's house.

"There's nothin' in here," his thin high voice tried to bellow down to his father.

His "There's" sounded normal. The Boy did not know that it had been captured by the cement. But by the time he heard his "nothin," the big-mouthed bridge-room had repeated "There's" because it didn't want it. "There's," was then amplified by the hard mouthed wall of the cave, and again by a cement-mouthed megaphone. It scared the bee-jeebers out of the Boy!

His sentence continued out of sheer inertia and its friend elapsed time. Bereft of his bee-jeebers, the Boy lost the end of his own sentence. It disappeared into the darkness never reaching the light of his father's day. Until, WHAM, the thunder of his words rolled out agin, a-scarin him, agin.

This was the first time the Boy stood in his own lightning and quaked in his own resulting thunder. Most future times he would not be quite so surprised.

Out of all those reverberations, his father finally said, "W-h-aaa-t?"

So the Boy reluctantly, and cautiously, said the same thing again, quietly.

"Swing around into the next room," Frank called back. "There's never anything in the skewback room."

The Boy crab-walked up the steep floor of the vacant room and grasped the edge of the vertical wall.

He looked down. The old dizzees came back. His hands were still shaking. The word fun was lost.

"Chew-ER: huh; ya; just swing around the edge," the Boy numb-bld.

He looked at the edge. His head eased out over the tilting floor that he squatted on. He looked around the edge with one eye. The other kept sneaking peeks at the rocks below.

He remembered snippets from the old family stories. "Your Uncle Gail was a real monkey when he went into the bridge. And Uncle Charlie was, too. I wasn't so good though," the Boy's father had said, "I wasn't as comfortable as they were."

"Comfortable," the Boy numb-bld, "come-fort-able?"

He looked at the little ledge at the wall's base. It was a stingy three inches.

Frank read the Boy's mind. "Face the wall. Slip your hand around the corner. Put your foot on the ledge and ease yourself around into the next room."

His father tried to be reassuring, but he was afraid for his boy because he remembered how he felt when he swung out over the river.

Without any thought as to where to put what foot, or how to lean, or which hand went where, or especially, how high he was, he monkneed his way around the wall, arriving in the higher room, and said without numb-ling, "I rilly am a monknee."

The room was like the first but it had a lower ceiling. This room is even more like a closet, a cave, a casket, the Boy thought.

As his eyes adjusted, again, the Boy saw the light shapes of pigeons toward the back of the room. Then, as he came closer, disappointment overcame him. There were strewn feathers in disjointed piles mixed with the hollow ends of gnawed bones. Otherwise there was nothing, nothing but pigeon crap.

"Rats," shouted the younger generation, not scaring himself quite as much this time, "There's nothing in this room, either, except scrufty feathers and dry bones."

"Rats," shouted the older generation meaning something extremely different. "Try the next room."

"W-h-aaa-t?" said the Boy stalling.

"It's always been that way in there. Did you see some skeletons that were all torn apart? The rats can get up there. Sometimes they catch the adults and eat them. That leaves the young birds to die of starvation."

"Gad-Zoo!" said the Boy.

He was ready to give up, to climb down.

His foot slipped on a wet softness on the floor.

"Crap," he said without thinking. It was probably the first time he had mumbled that word appropriately.

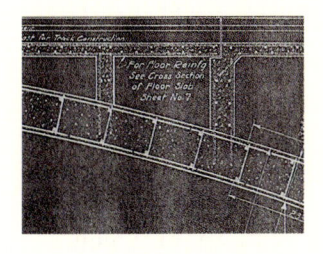

The monknee was in the next room almost before he thought of it. His nose arrived before he did. That nose could see the pigeon shit, could see the dead squabs before his eyes adjusted. When they did they saw what his ears had understood in family stories. He saw the skeletons in his family's closet.

He had always wondered what that saying meant. Now *voila*, he knew.

The mute carcasses were trapped in their own ribby cages. In death the birds had pulled their feathers around them, like blankets of eternity.

The Boy wondered how long they had been dead. One squab was completely dried. Its wing feathers were stripped of their delicate strands, stripped to bare quill, by decay.

What remained were the raw lines each bone and feather-bone drew in a cross-hatched portrait of its own death.

And not wanting to look further the Boy found that his eyes could not avoid seeing the other portraits in the avant-garde-gallery of the real surreal. One was a necklace of unarticulated neckbone-beads strung on invisible strands. Others were empty eggskulls.

The oversized beak of one such skull pointed deeper into the closet. Following the line of the pointer, the Boy saw a pigeon move. Hope sprang up but sunk again, as he realized that the bird was a dead dancer. A dumb-blind-dead dancer. Had Morris Graves seen the dead bird, he might have called it, "A well-known bird of the inner eye under the Last Avenue Bridge." The moose, the Moose Maudsley could have said, "Eat it little man."

The Boy related to the birds. He had seen himself in every mirror. He was as spare as they were. His head looked too big for his body. His nose had not yet grown past the stage of button-beak. Insufficient seemed his narrow neck. His cage of ribs trembled for oxygen in gasps of empathy. His shorts danced with the drum-sticks of his skin-knee pigeon legs. (If Charles

Darwin had visited the Galapagos Islands four million years ago, and if he had found this ancient boy-bird, he would have canceled his selection of selectivity.)

What the Boy was seeing on his squab adventure was contrary to all expectations. Events were occurring faster than descriptions. Bad was outweighing good. He was befuddled. His eye-mind was worrying up speed in a discovery that wanted to run in the opposite direction.

He picked up a feathery skeleton whose squab had taken a wrong turn at Hatching Junction where life and death crossed one another. He held nothing. What? Why? He put it down. He picked it up, again. What was this deception? How could it be so heavy yet weigh nothing? Some of his thinkers were out of whack. What was wrong with his boy-logic?

What does death want? Stealing life is enough! But stealing weight too? And where did the maggots go? What happens to life, at death time? When death comes, is any life left? How far is it from life to…

The Boy forgot where he was. He was on the verge of something…
His life and mind were on different expeditions. The stink of the closet was monkneeing around with him. He was flying a coop before pigeons could.

Frank shouted, "Are you OK up there? Is there something wrong?"

"No, its just more and more dead pigeons. Some are still dancing."

"Rats," said Frank, "en maggots. They've been poisoning pigeons downtown. Try the next cubby-hole."

The Boy was around the wall and into the next room faster than a weightless monk-nee. This monk-nee was not a dult but he was, by now, adroit.

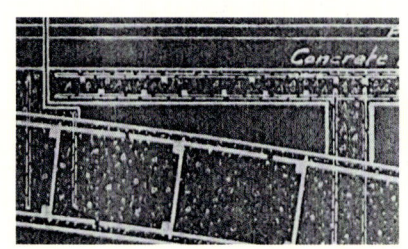

THE SQUABS

Even before he had time to brag, the Boy heard his own voice hollering (He scared himself again.) "They're here, they're here, three of them!"

He could see them huddled together as far back in the corner as they could get.

"OK," his father said while tying the rope to a gunnysack. He tossed the bag up toward the Boy.

On the third try the Boy caught the bag. He pulled up the dangling rope, untied it, and spread the bag. It smelled musty.

Now it was time to catch the pigeons.

He walked bandy-legged back into the dimness. He reached down to catch the first bird. Just as he touched it, the bird peeped loudly and jumped. The be-jeebers flew out of the Boy again. A coldness drenched him. He stood up. Without further thought he reached down and caught one of the other birds. It too, jumped, but not more than a fish might. That thought warmed the cold inside him.

A parent pigeon flew into the room nearly crashing into the Boy as it turned and fled on flapping wings.

With the squab cupped in his hands with its wings secured against flight, the Boy emerged from cold fright into a warmth of ecstasy.

Fun had begun, but it was marred by a suspicion that he may have squeezed the bird too hard when he got scared. The Boy eased his prize into the gunnysack, tied the rope and lowered it over the edge to his father. Frank spoke compassionately to the bird. He gently put the squab into the orange-crate and secured the chickenwire-wire.

An initiation was complete. Two generations were now on the same pleasant side of a rite. Both were united in mutual success. The warmth of the father was passed up to the son in an empty gunnysack. The generations were united in a long family tradition.

It was easy for the Boy to catch the other squabs. It was even easy for the Boy, as a rat, to scoot around the wall into the next room. This room was just the Boy's size. And there were more squabs to be caught and transferred into the orange-crate now even farther below. So confidence overcame fear of height.

As he caught several more squabs, he initiated himself into the First Class Squab Catching Club. "How many do we gotst now?" he called down to his dad.

He wanted more than whatever the number would be, but he also was becoming apprehensive about the next room. It was the keystone room, the last room, the top of the arch. It was very small.

He certainly would have to give up any of his monkney business and be Ratty-first-class if he was going into that rat hole. The ceiling of the Rat Hole was very low. Its tallest side was about twenty-four inches high. Its smallest side was too short for the Boy's anatomy to measure. "Rats could measure every inch, though," he thought. But, "the shortness of the room made the height of the bridge from the water," the Boy very consciously thought, "even higher!"

The fun-fear ratio was reaching a point of diminishing return. Yet, the Boy did inch into the highest room. He was immediately taken by the fact that the room was even smaller than it looked. And, and it was slickery—his ratty little hands and knees and even his tenny runners were pigeon shit.

Through the dim, dumb-dim light he could see a herd of pigeons in fort pigeon-haven. Several dults whipped past him clapping and slapping angrily as they broke free of the narrow space and plunged down into the sunlight. He was ascared, again.

As he crawled toward the squad of squabs cowering behind their outhouse, the feculence accumulated on his belly. He realized that this was the pigeons' main fort. They had built a large mound out of their only resource. It was positioned about three feet from the back wall. The grunge nearly reached to the ceiling.

He could see that the fortification of pigeon drop-goop was bird-designed to make the room too small for monknees. Like the trough on top of the Old Dam, it was a pit of nose gas. The mound was just too high. He could not crawl back any farther. His long bones were just too long. It was just too small for this rat.

He became a snake. He began to slither. "Uggggg! Even though I am a snake, I rilly wisht I had worn my shirt and long pants," the snake hissed, articulating the s soundsss fondly with his forked tongue.

The closer he got to the squabs the harder it was to move. There was no circulation. The air was so heavy that it had warped the floor and bent the ceiling. The stink was so dis-gust-sting that light could not penetrate it. "We're not a snake," the nose and the eyes kept saying. The putrid musk activated the Boy's tear ducts.

The nose and mouth said, "We're not a snake," again. "I'm a snake," the Boy hissed in return, "I'm a two-handed squab-catching snake." He demonstrated that by cantilevering his arms while he slithered forward. In a sudden strike he caught a squab. He was a success! He rilly was a snake!

He slithered backwards with no help from his hands. He WAS a success. He rilly was a snake. "Ooo-zho," the Boy said, as he reattached his legs when he neared the ledge.

It was a wonder-full bird, a positive hole in the brilliant brightness. It was purity. It was completely black. Perfection!

As the Boy again, he then lowered his prize down oh-so-carefully. His head hung out as he watched: until every perfect bird was in the orange-crate; until the chicken wire was secured.

Frank called up, "How many more squabs are there?"

"About ten," was the answer.

"Catch a few more. That will be enough," said Frank.

The snake wanted to catch all the pigeons but the nose thought that a few would be more than enough. Now, the snake eyes had to adjust, just had to, because selectivity entered the picture. Perhaps, the Boy thought, the snake should become a critic, a judge. Yes, a judge, from the All Iowa Fair, at Hike-On-Downs.

Now, the Boy must carefully consider each and every-every remaining squab: Did that one have a broken wing? Did that one have Droopy Sickness? Was that one, over there, a feather leg? Was there a red one in the crate already? The JUDGE considered each individual, ponderously. Then, wisely agreeing with the highest quality choices of the JUDGE, (the Boy,) the Boy completed HIS JUDGE-MENTS.

He lowered the birds.

It was decided by a nose that the Boy should scramble down to the rocks.

But that achievement was easier for Frank of The Rocks to say than for the Boy to accomplish, but he tried… He was now very good at rounding the walls of his rooms, as long as he was climbing upward and to his left, but now he needed to climb down and to the right. His right hand became his lead hand. OK, so what? He said: "Am I a monknee, or not? Monknees are am-be-deck-tru-s. And being a monknee, my feet are also hands."

His right front hand inquired around the end of the wall. It investigated while his left hind hand clutched the inside of the wall. The inquiring hand searched for one of the familiar notches against the opposite side of the wall. Such a handgrip had so kindly helped him when he ascended the sections of the bridge's arch. This inquiry offered no such help as he tried to descend. In fact, the monknee's hand was very surprised to discover no help at all from the descending arch of the bridge.

Slowly, but surely, his hand began to ss-slip-p…

Faster than Charles Darwin's wildest dreams, the Boy's realization sliding with his own weight toward an imminent fall, sent evolution faster than lightning back into being the eye of a boy's foot. The foot was discovering many things in its slow downward slide but what it wanted was imagination, the imagination of instincts that were monknee and boy.

An inner eye saw him safely beside his father who was a rock among the rocks.

Without looking or thinking back, the Boy spotted his magnificent Blacky. "OH, thank goodness," he cooed, "you sure look good!"

His father carried the crate, but not carefully enough, toward home. No human could carry the precious crate with enough dignity to satisfy the Boy who pranced beside his father. Even though the Boy didn't think of himself as a pigeon yet, everyone else thought he must be one because of the pigeon-shit from the top of his head and his poop-deck down to the poopy bottom of his tenny-runners.

This small parade marched from the First Avenue Bridge right over to the new coop on Summer Street. The Boy was all of the animals who had helped him catch the squabs. The Pallas eye of his mother missed not one single detail when he, they, smartly passed her on her reviewing stand, the back porch.

The Old Dam, had first watched when the Boy climbed into the belly of his best friend, the First Avenue Bridge. Then the Dam could only listen. Then he had watched, again, as the Boy descended to the river's rocks. The memory of the homecoming parade warmed him.

The Old Dam smiled through his listening as the Boy tenderly put the last of the pigeons to roost in their new coop.

THE LOUSES

As it turned out, the pigeon parade officially ended Frank's vacation. It was Friday afternoon at 3:30. The weekend and the big game now teased out ahead of the family and the Boy. All day long he had been having trouble with his underpants. Every place they touched, it itched like crazy. He finally told his mother.

She immediately thought that the problem was lice from the pigeons. She flew into a tizzy, "The family is lousy, oh no, lousy!"

While she raged, the Boy pulled down the upper edge of his undershorts to scratch one of the places that was itching. Nona, observed the row of welts around the band. "Chiggers," she said. "Thank god, we don't have lice." Her relieved mind had just switched from an unacceptable social malady to a familiar and tolerable one, one that was never so bad as to require professional treatment back when she was on the farm.

To the Boy, the feisty itch, itched and itched just the same.

But Nona's relief from this escape would change later after the Boy's sister Beverley was born. She played beauty shop with the neighbors; she would not be playing later, however, with the head-lice she brought home. When that happened, Gramma stepped forward and lined up all the kids. She saw to it that everyone was treated. That memorable remedy involved a kerosene shampoo for every kid's hair.

Another social relative of the louse that fascinated the Boy, was ringworm. This constantly circulated through the schools. The school's prisoners with this defeugalty, could be recognized by the worm-trails on their shaven heads. The Boy studied these heads from a safe distance. They were colorfully painted or plastered in the hope that the medicine would follow the worm-excavated trails in the skin, to the tunneling worms themselves. Sometimes the Boy could see that the worms, that were not really worms, had been caught and killed in their tracks. It was fascinating.

All of the ring-worm-a-lings were demeaned into wearing women's stockings for head-dress dressings. "Oh, look who came to school today, King Sissy-stocking. Did you come with Queen Baldy?" Leo might have said. The Boy told both Ronnie and Leo that if HE ever got the ring-a-ling, HE would start toward school but HE would never arrive there until HE was cured.

Even being caught for hooky would be better than biting the worm by having to go to school in a Sissy King-stocking. The Boy confided that he would not be able to face tormentors like himself. Of course, that admission did not dull the devastating words sharpened by what he considered to be a playful tongue.

During one worm-a-demic, dick-tech-tive nurses moved into the basement room of Fillmore where the class had "Ya walk/ ya walk/ ya walk/ don't talk/" made their way down to watch the movie about Old Shakey-spears.

There they stood in a long line that reached out into the hallway and even up a few of the steps. The school nurse, wearing rubber gloves, placed each student's head under a strange goose-necked lantern. The worry-wrinkles on her face made it look like she was cultivating a crenulated contagion.

It was verrry mysterious in that dark room. The overall effect was one of hot pink and cold purple. When the head of each schoolmate was passed under the light, the Boy hoped that something awefuller than the worm would be revealed. The Boy's imagination went wild with what that might look like. He also feared that the vilest head discovered might be his own.

He had a good imagination but he wanted to see a revealing that was twice as bad as anything he could invent. He anticipated that the lights might discover purple-pink maggots with yellow-green spots and huge teeth.

The Boy didn't conform to the in-line march— "You walk/ you walk/ you walk don't talk/" when it headed back to his classroom. He hung back in an itchy hope that someone's thinker-top would trip the fancy light's fancy.

When the School Principal's wizened hand caught up with the scruff of the Boy's neck, it needed no words. It half lifted and half shepherded him away from the education he so desired to one he was not interested in.

That was a good year. Impetigo came to school: so did mumps, chickenpox, measles and many of their friends. It was a profitable year for tonsil surgeons.

It was the year of the mumbles and, and the craving for iced cream. Several girls got romantic fever. They had to stay in bed, some for as long as a year.

On the way home from school that year he playfully pushed his friend's head into an innocent snow pile by his front porch. Unfortunately, the friend's cracked and bruised head bled to the doctor at St. Luke's Hospital because it had found a cement wall just under the snow. The doctor spilled to his friend's parents. The parents informed their son that he was the Boy's former friend.

The Boy was so sorry that he became forgetful while he was launching an ice-ball he manufactured by freezing it under a different friend's fort-porch. They had designed it to be used in their wars on girls, especially against girls with romantic fever who would not play with them. Unfortunately he threw one of the ice balls just when a cop car cruised past. The police didn't understand the symptoms of the Boy's romantic fever but revealed the value of the status of former friends.

"Chiggers," Nona mumbled, again, as she walked to the kitchen stove. She put on a big kettle of water. "Time for a bath," she said to the Boy. When the water was finally hot, she poured it into the claw-foot bathtub and then slowly added the cold tap until it was just right. The Boy climbed in, protesting, but actually enjoying. Nona stood at the medicine chest. "Chiggers," escaped from her mouth again, while she scratched through the cabinet's mysteries.

In a malicious and superior tone once again, she mercilessly loaded the little word, "Lice!" in a way she wouldn't have loaded her Clydesdale. "Lydia Pinkum's, alum, styptic pencil, I wonder if Lydia Pinkum's would work? Campho Phenique, Mentholatum, rubbing alcohol, Vaseline, Mercurochrome, Murine Eye Drops, no. Coal tar, would that be good?" Moving Carter's Little Liver's—"No." Moving the eye cup, the camphor—"Nope," the Milk of Magnesia, "Na," the Ex-Lax, "Ah ha… HA ha!, that might be good."

What Nona decided upon, with lice still itching her thinking, was to use the Campho Phenique, the Mentholatum ointment and the rubbing alcohol. Then, while he scrubbed, she decided that the Menthol and alcohol would be enough.

"OK," she said, "Get out of the tub and stand on this towel." He did. She said, "Rub this Menthol over the whole area. Now, make little mounds over each bite." The Boy carefully applied the salve. It was cold but it didn't hurt. "OK, now rub this alcohol over everything."

Before the Boy could quite finish the application, he was jumping and yelling because of the chemical reaction. "Yeow!" he yelled. "It burns. Ow, ouch. It's terrible!" he danced.

"Jump back into the tub," his mother suggested. He did. "Yeowee," he yelled, even louder, "Holy balls," blurted from his lips as the heat from the alcohol was sealed in by the water. The pain concentrated in the worst possible place.

"What is it?" Nona yelled, although she was standing right next to the Boy.

"It's the nuts!" he wailed. "They're burning off."

They each grabbed for the towel but the Boy was by far the quickest. He immediately began to rub as roughly and as ten-der-ly as he could. Nona stood outside the pain, but in the center of the empathy. She was stooped-over, babbling mumbles, as she helplessly held the other end of the towel.

It was a conundrum.

The Boy's end of the towel converted the open fire into a smolder, then into the heat of an oven, still cooling, after baking. The towel's work did not stop the dance but it did diminish its tempo.

Dried and partially dressed, the Boy reached for the heap on the floor that was his pigeon shit shorts. His mother's hand, however, guided it instead to the clean pair of long pants on the chair.   She lifted the wretched shorts with the tip of her index finger, condemned the offenders, dropping them into the pile of other dirty clothes and slamming the wicker hamper closed. She would clean up their act on Monday morning when she did the laundry.

THE GAMES

The Boy sat in the back seat of the black 1931 Model A Ford. He had been in the front seat but then he had vaulted back and forth several times. It was hot, so he cranked down all the windows.

Well, he didn't just sit, he fidgeted, he scratched, and he wiggled. He wanted to get going. Where were they? He wanted to get to Ellis Park for the big softball game.

Finally, his mother came out; she got in the back too, and placed the baby between them. Frank soon followed. He drove them over to pick up the Moose, who lived way out on the other side of town, about two miles away.

As soon as they pulled up to the curb, Moose leaped out of the house. He had his cleats in one hand and his glove in the other.

118

"Sooo, you came to pick up the star did ya?" he bellowed. He jumped into the front, but he didn't close the door. He relaxed into his seat and jammed his foot into the hinge of the door. His elbow draped out the window.

The Boy immediately catapulted to his special spot between the two men. From there, he could smell one of his favey-favor-it smells, the skin on his father's arm after it had been tanned in sunshine.

Frank drove away. They stopped for gas on Center Point Road and the men swung out of the car. The attendant started to hand pump gas up into the glass holding-tank on the top of the gas dispenser. He stopped pumping because neither Frank nor Moose had told him how much gas they wanted. His job was to pump the proper amount needed for the sale. Moose reached over and unscrewed the gas cap between the two halves of the hood saying, "Well I guess we need to fill 'er up with ten cents worth, since that's all you are pumping up for us!" Moose's teeth were still smiling, "Can you run on fumes with these gravity feeds?"

Frank said, "Put in two dollars' worth." The man pumped that amount up into the glass tank then drained that gas down into the car.

In order to get back across the river they had to pass Cedar Lake. There was a low area where the road was only dirt. Big puddles seemed to be crossing the road like turtles would, to join the lake. About a block before they got to the puddles, Moose clandestinely reached his left foot up under the dash, where the gas line fed down to the carburetor. He cleverly kicked the valve shut. The car started to misbehave. A half block later it showed its total disobedience by stopping right in the middle of the largest puddle.

"I don't know what's wrong," Frank worried.

"Maybe water splashed up on the magneto," the Moose conjectured in a very helpful way.

The Boy squirmed. Nona was calm, and so was the baby. Moose jumped right out of the car as if there were no puddle. He lifted his side of the hood and fiddled under there.

Frank wasn't far behind. He had, first, taken off his shoes and rolled up his pants. He fiddled under his side of the hood. They checked the plugs, spark plug wires, air filter, carb...

Moose closed his hood and came over to Frank's side. "I think I got it," he said. "I'll jump in, you crank."

Moose climbed under the wheel and opened the gas valve with his foot. He set the gas and the spark. "Frank - Frank turned the crank," Nona said as he turned the crank. It started.

Everyone was happy, more especially the Moose who gave up his seat to the Frank. They were off, again, for the game. They went down the viaduct past Danceland, where Uncle Roger worked. Moose fanned his door to make it seem like the fart he had perpetrated was raunchier than it was.

Just before they got to the F Avenue Bridge, a Moose hoof fandangoed the valve, again.

This time they stopped right in the middle of the bridge. Cars honked. Men enunciated strings of words that the Boy mumbled in an effort to increase his vocabulary. When his mother voiced a protesting concern, he volunteered that he had heard almost all those words before. This increased, rather than diminished, her concern.

The Boy jumped out of the door Moose left dangling. He wanted to see if the fish were biting and who was fishing from the Old Dam. Moose couldn't find the defeugalty as quickly this time. The men fiddled and fiddled. When the moment came for Frank to crank, Moose did not turn the valve back on. Frank-Frank turned the crank for a long tiring time. His arm started to get sore after the crank caught and nearly threw him for a loop.

In the back seat, Nona decided that it was a good time to change the baby's diaper. The honks from the cars didn't seem to bother her much.

Uncle Charlie, who was fishing, came over to say that nothin' was bitin'. He asked, "What time does the game start?" Frank moaned, "I hope we're not late." Moose, who often displayed something far beyond a healthy disrespect, said, "Hell, there's plenty of time."

When Charlie left, Nona sang to the baby,

> *"Down by the bridge*
> *In an itty-bitty pool*
>
> *Swam two boy fishes*
> *And a Franky fish, too.*
> *Stop said the momma fish*
> *Stop, if you can.*
> *So they swam and they swam*
> *Right over the dam.*
>
> *Singing bim, bamb, batta-waa tumb*
> *Singing bim, bamb, batta-waa tumb*
> *They swam and they swam*
> *Back over the dam.*
>
> *The two little fishes*
> *Went out on a lark*
> *All of a sudden*
> *They met a Moose shark*
>
> *Swim, said the mamma fish*
> *Swim if you can.*
> *So they swam and they swam*
> *Right over the dam*
>
> *Singing bim, bamb, batta-wa tumb*
> *Singing bim, bamb, batta-wa tumb*
> *They swam and they swam*
> *Back over the dam."*

"Din" Nona thought she heard the baby say, so she did sing it again, and din again and a din...

She tickled the baby and rocked him as she sang.

Frank groaned, "Moooose? will you crank for awhile?" Moose said, "OK," at the same time he opened the valve again. Nona happened to notice what he was doing with his foot. She kiddingly cuffed him on the shoulder, and giggled, pointing. The car started on the first crank of the Moose. Moose horsed, "I guess you're not as strong as I am," as he hurried back into the car right behind the Boy.

The car ran just fine after that, but who knows how many stops it would have taken, had Nona not observed the prankster in action.

"Whata 'bout the game?"

Nona interrupted her singing of Bim, bamb, botta-watum ... near the Mosque. At a corner grocery she quietly recited a little ditty to the baby. She said it just loud enough so that anyone paying attention to her might hear.

Dean, Dean, made a machine
Frank, Frank, turned the crank
Joe, Joe made it go
Just because Steven was leav'n.

Frank, Frank, turned the crank
Pop? Pop? Who made it stop?
A goose-goose, or maybe, A moose?
Just because Steven was leav'n…

Dean, Dean…

Of course, no one but the baby was paying any attention. As they got closer to the park all the men folk seemed to want to talk at the same time.

But, when they reached the end of Ellis Boulevard, Moose Maudsley's left elbow nudged the Boy's ribs, while his right index-finger and lips silently said shhhhh—to the Boy. Moose's naughty left hand, then, snuck down by the Boy's feet and fiddled with the screw at the base of the gearshift lever.

When Frank was preparing to shift gears and turn right at the main diamond, however, Moose handed him that shifter saying, "Did anyone lose this? Do you need this for anything?" He acted as if he was about to throw it away.

Frank grabbed it.

Moose mooed and bawled out his laughter as Frank tried to steer, brake, push in the clutch, and restore the gearshift all at the same time. Frank let the car coast to a stop in the bushes behind deep right field. He jumped from the running board and chased the Moose across the field and into the dugout swearing in angry laughter.

But the Boy missed the last response by Frank to Moose-foolery because he had gone immediately to the car's trunk as it came to a stop. His mind was elsewhere, like his body soon would be. He removed the orange crate and his fish pole and…

The dugout was full of camaraderie, and general bullshit was in progress. Razzing was rampant. Moose had a bottle of beer sticking out of each of his hip-pockets. Where they came from was anybody's guess. One of the bottles was already opened.

He perched his ass on the dugout bench as be bent over while putting on his spikes. The fact that not one drop of his beer spilled did not escape the notice of Wood Chuck Polansky. He tried to encourage the Moose into a friendly spill with a sneaky nudge, but the oom-Moo was ready. Moose

123

toasted the Chuck with his bottle while rising to roast himself. "To the Moose-est, the big-gest, the most-est—the great-est, soft baller in the world."

He took a deep swig.

Then, in a sudden mock pitch, he sent the rest of his beer spewing from his foaming bottle into a half circle libation. For an instant it was a rainbow that fizzed in the dust just outside the dugout. With the attention of teammates, fans and foes alike, he strutted the silliest strut out to the pitcher's mound for warm-ups.

Frank hunkered in the dust, behind the plate, to catch the fastest mouth and one of the bestest pitchers in the league.

Nona, with the baby, watched from the blanket she had spread in right field, but she couldn't hear the players' banter. They were just inside the shrubbery and encircling parked cars. The cars seemed to be watching the game over the top of a hedge.

Nona giggled at the antics of the Moose. She liked his "Cute little Moose-ass," and even his beer bottle jokes. Frank and the Moo, the Maud, both "Looked great," she thought, in their white duck trousers and their dark Witwer's Grocery Store shirts. Their high socks made their legs look like the necks of Canada Geese, upside-down. When Moose raised his cleated-foot during a pitch, it looked, for-all-the-world, like one goose had teeth.

Moose finished his other beer when Iowa Man(ufacturing) was on the field for warm-ups.

During the third inning the score was still tied 0-0. Moose was doing well. Frank's right hand was beginning to turn red from catching Moose's fastest pitches. His big finger escaped from the punishment through the hole hacked in the back of the mitt.

Frank kidded every hitter that approached the plate. Frank remembered aloud every error they had made when they had been at bat before and every one they had made in the field, too. He asked them innocent questions about "...their problems." He was so sympathetic. He was a man of empathy.

"Did you hurt yourself when you swung and missed that curve? Next time let me know if you're going to try to steal by sliding home, I'll get out of your way. I see they're short of men over at the Man. Have you ever tried two bats?"

When Frank wasn't a psychiatrist to the Man in front of him, he was a teacher for the man in the stripped shirt that stood behind him. "Bawl two," the Ump would say. Frank would say, "What?" "Bawl three," the Ump might bawl. "Ya-know," Frank said, "There was an ump out here last week who called that same pitch a strike. Interesting isn't it? He might have been right, too."

"Stee-rike one," said the Ump through his mask. "You're right," said Frank. "Keep up the good work." In the third inning, another Man's man tried to steal home without warning Frank. It caused quite a collision. The Umps, "Uuuurrr-Out!" cold could have completed the sentence. The Man's man seemed to prefer lying in the dust near the unreached plate. His recovery was far too slow, in Moose time. He said, "Oh, hell, just let him lay there and bleed. Let's play ball."

The Man's man came-to just in time to hear the Moose's heckle. He became so enraged that he jumped up and charged toward the Moose-mound hollering that Moose was full-a-shit. Apparently the man HAD actually been knocked unconscious because when he attempted to rush toward the Moose he actually ended up running in a curved line that terminated in the arms of Wood Chuck Polansky at first base.

The Chuck kept asking the man, "Are you all-right? Are you all-right?" The Man's man answered like a man, "Ya, I'm all right now, thanks, but just let me get at that damned Moose. The field seems to be holding still now. It sure was turning just after I hit that wall in front of the plate."

The Wood Chuck chuckled as he helped the Man's man to the Man's dugout. The Moose came over to help, saying, "Sorry, I didn't know ya was rilly hurt. Buy ya a beer after the game." Sometimes a Moose's mouth runs faster than a moose, he added to himself as he walked back to the mound.

Later, every time one of his teammates struck out, or grounded out, Moose Maudsley mooed, "Let me bat." The other players knew how good-a hitter he was, especially against the best pitchers. He usually got two or three hits, but that still didn't make up for his mouth.

"Too bad I can't be up to bat all the time," grumbled the Moose from the dugout. Then he hollered, "What's wrong with you, gettin' tired?" to the Man's pitcher as he walked Frank. His large moose lips really mumbled and chewed his words when his next man struck out, "Aww, I wisht I could bat all the time."

In the sixth inning, the formerly injured Man's man came to bat. The first Moose pitch was a fastball. It stung Frank's hand before the breeze of the Man's wiffff, of intended revenge, stirred the leaves on the trees.

"Thanks," said Frank, "that breeze you stirred up sure helped cool my hand." The second pitch was outside and away, Moose's upshoot speeder had missed the plate. "Bawl two."

Frank said to his two cozy companions, "Wow, wasn't that one purddy? You prolly couldn't see it because of all that steam comin' out of my mit. It was perfect! Wanna check the ball, Ump? It might have singed seams. Wanna warm your hands on my hot-pad Clyde?" (All the Man's men were named Clyde.)

The next pitch was released in an exact duplicity of the Moose's windmill-fastball delivery. The Moose made a complete, speedy, three-hundred-and-sixty-degree circle of his almost invisible arm and underhandedly released the most perfect high arching s-l-o-w-b-a-l-l that could be thrown through the gravity of this earth.

The batter swung at the ball before it left Moose's hand. He then had the privilege of watching it as it ascended to its apex and descended through Moose's hearty laugher… …he was so frustrated that he swung again and missed again as it finally bounced up from the middle of the rubber home plate into Frank's mitt.

Frank let out a terrific holler, "Owwwwwwww," and danced a painful dance in the dust, shaking his hurted hand, while the ump shouted, "Stee-rike two," that was heard the compass 'round, followed by a chuckled whisper into the laughs coming from the stands, "Steeerike three."

The Moose yelled in to the batter, "OK, so you liked that one, did ya? Wanna-nother-one-jus-like-it?" The batter did, did indeed, and he said so, with certain tight-lipped swear words under his breath. Those words were only pinch-hitters, though, for the real, the gross, the foul-ball words he used at the factory. The factory work words were sizzlers.

The Moose thought the situation through and through. He knew what the Man's man would be thinking. Soooo, the Moose threw that exact pitch again. It was difficult to tell when the man realized that it was not the extremely fast pitch he had come to expect—the one he planned to punish with his anger the one he planned to blast across the street for a home run.

The Man's man was so frustrated when he saw the ball still floating in the air after his first swing missed that he danced forward, swinging, and missing, a second time. He dipped his bat into the dust and mentally struck the ball again. The ball was an ellusive piñata keeping all the candy for someone else's successful swing. He drug his bat, like a useless tail, through the Talcum powder dust toward his dugout. When the ball cuddled into Frank's pillow and the bum-pire shouted, "Stee-rike three. Stee-rike four. You're out—you're out," in a way that was v-e-r-y satisfying, Frank turned the crank by rifling the ball back to the Moose as hard as he could.

Moose turned his attention to digging holes and practiced making dust devils on the mound.

The next Man to bat was a real man. He blasted a home run that made Moose's Maudsley tongue shrivel.

The last Man grounded out to end the inning, 0-1.

Frank came to the plate with a bat in his hand. He stepped up to the plate…

𝒥𝒲

About an hour earlier, The Boy walked over to the golf course. It had been a sight to see him leave the car. Following his inner plan, he carried the orange crate and his fish pole. His plan was original, like soooo many of his other plans, but it had been coaxed into existence by family stories.

He hurried awkwardly along until he crossed the seventh green and headed for the dinky crick that crossed the seventh and eighth hole fairways. Upon arrival he was dis-tracted by a leopard frog. It was a most Beauty-full beast, soooo shiny slick. Its sheen started under the skin of its teeth then bumped over its eye bulges. Its shine glided through the angular shoulders and slid between the sharpish hips. The sheeny green shine meandered just like the little crick when it got to the fatted and folded hind legs. The delicate leopard had used up all of its spots when it got to its wonderfully delicate toes and their ingeniously designed webs. It would have borrowed some spots from its tail but it couldn't find one.

The Boy thought, "This guy is made to jump! Look," he said to himself, "its heart is beating in its throat, or is it swallowing?"

The Boy eased forward on his haunches, his hand gathered itself into the stealth and the patience of a snake getting ready to strike, when he was distracted by his first objective.

A perfect chipmunk scurried into his peripheral vision and chip-monkneyd its way into the center of the Boy's attention.

The little rascal ran into one of the holes in the crick bank. The Boy hurried to the hole while he unreeled line from his fish pole. He made a little noose that he placed around the opening of the hole.

He backed away and lay flat on the ground. As he waited, his eyes wouldn't hold still. They did not completely watch the chipmunk hole. Instead the disobedient eyes wandered around until they found the frog. How could they miss? It must have hopped over to see what the Boy was doing. Leeper was only about three feet away from his head, just out of reach.

The Boy didn't want to catch the frog, not right then, but his hands did. They succeeded! They put the frog into the orange crate. When they did so, the frog peed on them. "Piss on it, little man," the Moose in the Boy laughed. As he fiddled with the chicken wire trying to secure the lid, his foot caught in the fishing line. That accidentally pulled the noose out of the chipmunk's door.

The Boy mumbled in Moose-talk as he fixed the noose and laid back down to watch for the striped tiger to stick his head out of his hole.

"I can remember everything that I've been taught," he thought. Then he reviewed it again, "When the striper sticks its head out of the hole, don't pull right away. You'll strangle the little rascal. Wait until it comes out a little further. Wait until its front feet come out," his Uncle Charlie had said. "Then jerk it in. But watch out for the teeth. For little rookies, they sure have b-i-g teeth," he had grinned the grunt while making his own teeth look v-e-r-y big!

These and many other gems about tigers went through the Boy's mind as he waited in an almost dream. He conjured the little guy into a cage turning a wire wheel around-and-around as it ran so fast he couldn't see its feet.

The single-mindedness of chiggers that lived in his skin kept reminding the Boy that he "should" scratch. He had to roll one way and another to accomplish the proper responses without using his hands, which might scare the little-munker. He had watched lying dogs make similar movements. It helped, but failed to satisfy.

"Try not to scratch," memory of his mother repeated. Yet, the more he tried not to, the more he scratched.

Then, just a few feet away, lodged deep in the mudded-face of the crick-bank, he spotted the white dimples of what might be a golf ball, buried by a hard drive. True, he might have thought that he could wait until after he caught the chipper. Yes, he could investigate then. … But since the chipmunk hadn't shown up yet, he reasoned, he'd have time to check this out, now. He started to crawl over to the ball, but his foot nudged the pole and the noose escaped the hole again.

It was a golf ball, with only one small cut in it. It was a Titleist 3, too. He could get ten cents for that one at the Pro Shop. He cleaned it in the crick and wiped it on his pants leg. Thinking these long pants are good for somethin', he put the ball into his pocket.

Fifty or a hundred chiggers, or ten clock minutes later, he saw the mighty tiger lift its head. The Boy held his line like he did when a fish was nibblin. He waited. The little shit seemed to be looking right at him. It seemed suspicious. It looked all around… and… Out-came-the-front-legs!

As if a fish had just bit hard, he yanked the line and at the same time lifted his pole high. He had one, a beauty. The stripper swam through the air. The Boy lowered the tiger into the cage with the leopard. He secured the chicken-wire wire.

"But should I untie the little fellow?" the Boy thought. "It might get out if I reach into the cage. And those big teeth?" Look at those muscles in its cheeks.

As if in answer, the frantic chipmunk jumped swiftly from one side of the cage to the other. It even crawled upside down on the chicken wire lid. Then, with those ferocious t-e-e-t-h, it bit through the fish line in a single snappy chomp.

The Boy glanced at his fingers.

As close as he could get to running, the Boy then headed toward his father's CCC army-blanket that he knew would be spread on the grass in right field. He ran right across the games' outfield where the Church League was playing. Most of the players called out teasing remarks, "I know a place where you can buy a boat if you want to fish in this deep grass." "How many oranges did you catch today?" "If a fly-ball comes your way, catch it in that crate. Then we'll call this the Orange Bowl Game." "Are the fish biten' out there in center field?" "Have you tried that lobster pot down in the river yet?" "That's the skinniest fungo I've ever seen."

One player yelled out some words that the Boy didn't think he'd use in church.

Just as the Boy returned to the CCC army blanket that Nona was sitting on with Steven in right field, Frank stepped to the plate, with one away, in the bottom of the seventh. Through excellent acting, he attained the exact posture that The Babe had used in a newsreel he had seen at the Iowa Theater. Frank, The Babe, pointed to the outfield, indicating exactly where he intended to hit the ball for a home run. Babe pounded his bat on home plate, then took the first pitch. "Huh," he called out to the pitcher, "can't you throw any faster than that?" "Stee-rike one." said the bum-pire.

Babe stepped out of the box and took a terrific practice cut. He smeared dust on his hands and rubbed it into the handle of the bat. Some of the dust "inadvertently" drifted into the eyes of the catcher and his masked companion, King-O-Sobby.

Then he spit both right and left. He dug in!

The pitcher delivered a knuckler. The batter took a beautiful cut, a terrific ripple. "Stee-rike two," could be heard as a breeze sprang up in the infield. The infielders moved back a couple of steps. Babe growled as he punished the plate with his timber.

Moose mumbled, "I wish I could pinch-hit for everybody." The pitcher reached down into his glove for his fastest fast-ball. He delivered it right down the middle. A perfect home run pitch, if ever there was one.

The infields leaned back on the cleats of their heels, in self-protection. Then Frank pulled a perfect bouleversement; he laid down a classic bunt.

He ran…

He lounged on the first sack…

He hiked up his pants…

He spit…

He scratched…

The embarrassment then finally reached the infielders. They all wished they had been outfielders. The outfielders, confident that they would have made the out, wished they had been infielders.

Nona and the Boy were so proud!

The Boy was so excited by that neat bunt that he almost forgot to say, "Mom, Mom, look what I got. A Tiger and a Leopard!" She looked into the cage with one eye, and saw the hyper chipmunk and the docile frog as the other eye watched the next batter sacrifice.

Frank advanced to second.

"Two away!" the infielders shouted to one another as they threw the ball around the bases. "Easy hitter," they bantered as a Moose meandered toward the keystone.

"Do I get to bat just now?" he muttered.

Nona was having a hard time trying to keep her attention on the Boy and his brother who needed to have his diapers changed, Frank on second base, the Leopard and the Tiger in the cage and a Moose up to bat.

Everything focused, however, when the pitcher delivered his first, his fastest and his last pitch.

Moose helped the ball take a tour of the vicinity. It buzzed the infielders. It waived at the outfielders. It pleasantly looked down at the lights in left field. It enjoyed the panoramic vista. It looked both ways before crossing the street. Then it weeded the neighbor's garden.

The game was over Witwers won 2-1.

The team drove to the drive-in on the corner of F Avenue and Ellis Boulevard. That's where they almost found enough beer to water a moose.

Moose bought a round of shells for the men from the Man. Moose was the Boulevardier, the man-about CR-town.

The player from the Man team who had collided with the Frank at home plate accepted a second shell from Frank. (He was starting to feel much better.)

He told Frank that he sure would like to see that slow ball float up to him again. Frank replied, "Don't worry Clyde… you'll see it again …in your dreams."

Later, the fishermen on the dam could hear singing coming from a Model A that was crossing the F Avenue Bridge, traveling east. It was circuitously taking the two heroes home. After dropping the Moose at his house it turned and crossed the bridge again. With the baby crying the singing parts that the heroes, Nona, and the Boy were singing…

> *The two little fishes*
> *Swam home in the dark*
> *Swam home from a game*
> *In El-lis Park*
>
> *Sleep said the mamma fish*
> *Sleep if you can*
> *But they swam and they swam*
> *Right over the dam.*
> *Singing bim, bamb, batta-wa tumb*

Singing bim, bamb, batta-wa tumb
They swam and they swam
Right into the dam.

The Old Dam was listening with River-tear's in his eyes.

AND THEN

It was one of those last-time pushing, and first-time pulling, deals of life. The Boy had to decide, and he did! "I will never stop being the Boy! College will not snatch that away from me!"

And the Old Dam said, "I will always be here as your anchor. Remember, your College is on the banks of the Red Cedar River, our…"

$$\int \heartsuit \mathcal{U}$$

The Boy was going fishing on the apron of the Old Dam (…and yes, he was saying his goodbyes!)

The Boy smiled as he turned at the "Best Lumberyard by a Dam Site," then he nodded thanks to the plank, said good afternoon to the steel boatlocks that were patiently rusting while waiting for friendly chipmunk and rat conversations.

He then made a left turn and slid down the ramp that was covered with slippery green slime, knowing how lucky it was he had arrived at the flat bottom of the fish ladder. He slud over the edge and into the water. "Oh oh-so-cold!" The water reached above his swimsuit. He turned east and stepped up onto the Dam's apron.

The water there was just below his knees. Now he was in a comfortably friendly and safe place. He slowly walked over to pier One. Two. Three! His minnow bucket was nudging him along. At pier Four swirls of current wrapped around him issuing hellos and… be-care-fuls?

The Boy arrived at the tongue of the over-ledge of his fishing hot-spot. This is where danger lived!

The Boy turned and waded toward the F Avenue Bridge. His toes quit measuring in feet and nervously started measuring in inches. Then the slippery ledge told the Boy, in no uncertain terms, BACK UP!"

At this very spot, years ago, the Old Dam had agreed to let the River erode some of its concrete real-estate. *SO* the River sculpted a wonderfully perfect fishing hole with the help of ferocious Floods.

On this most wonderfull-est of august August days, the Old Dam let his friend the River slide over him, just right! Perfect for fishing!

Oh, is that Miss Darling crossing the Bridge in that white doily dress?

The Boy hooked a minnie minoso to his hook and threw his line just beyond the underwater drop-off. Perfect. The bobber drifted toward the Bridge. …and *voila* a bite immediately turned into a fish on the stringer. It was a catfish-fish that soon became two stringers full-a fish, tied to his belt.

The Boy's minnie bucket nudged the Boy's leg saying: "Here's another minnie!"

But the Boy wasn't paying any attention because he was heading toward the east bank of the River. When he got there he looked for a place to hide his stringers of fish. He left the river and went to the usual spot where his dad would be parking the car.

It was almost 3:30 when Frank got off work at P. M. Lattner's where he welded boilers. The Boy liked the smell of sweat mixed with smoked welding on his dad's arms. Grabbing his pole and tackle box, Frank hurried to follow the Boy to that favey-favorite spot.

Not fast enough. They were on the apron, but… the stringers and their hidden fish were missing?

135

The mystery was waiting for understanding.

Finally there were two fishermen standing together on the apron. It cannot be told how many fish they caught. But they filled five stringers.

Uncle Charlie might have reported to a game warden, "Naa, Nutin' bitin' today."

Others came and they "Swam and they swam Right over the dam."

The Boy said good, good-byes to his mom and dad, his good Old Dam, the River, his F Avenue Bridge and the warm, worn bricks of Summer Street.

The Boy swam upstream into another life on the same River, at a Cedar falls where…

> He studied and he studied
> And he fished and he fished
> Right over the dam,
>
> Said the Young Old Dam.

…and his father's question still needs to be answered: "What will we do when all of the water goes downstream?"

R.S.-16   5/20   JPage '64

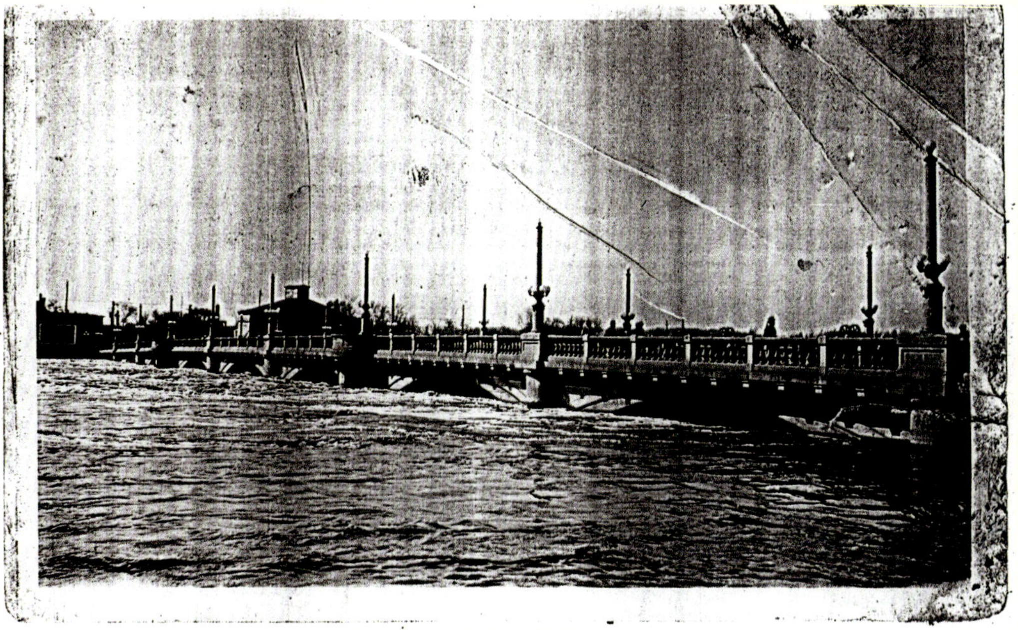

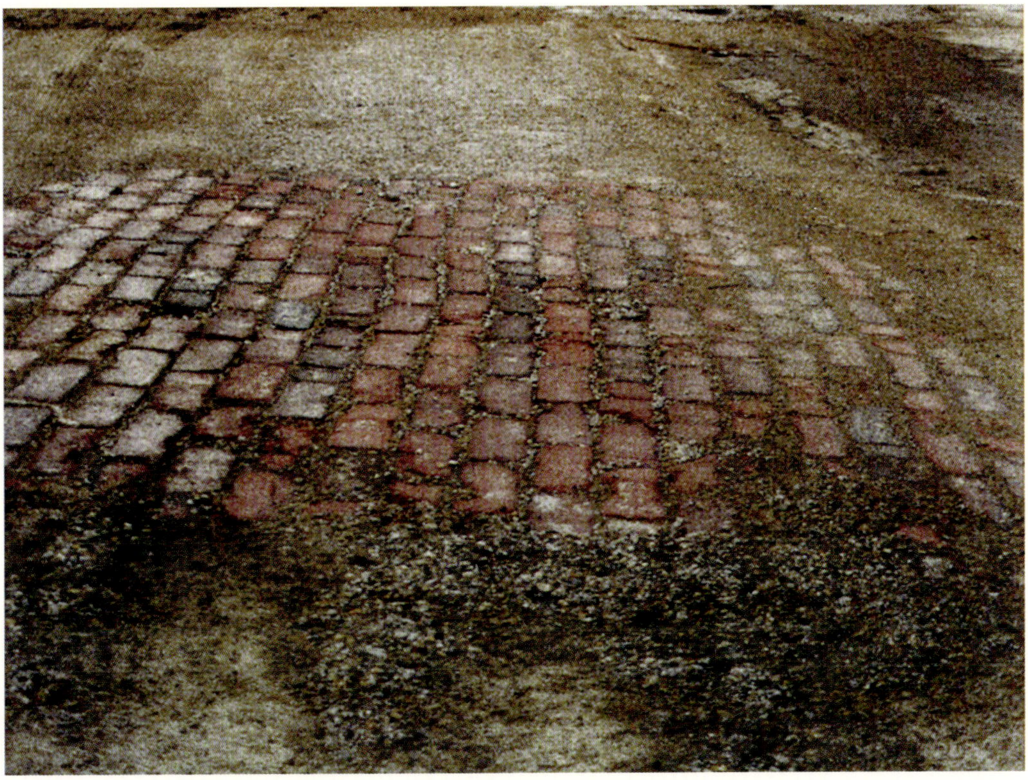

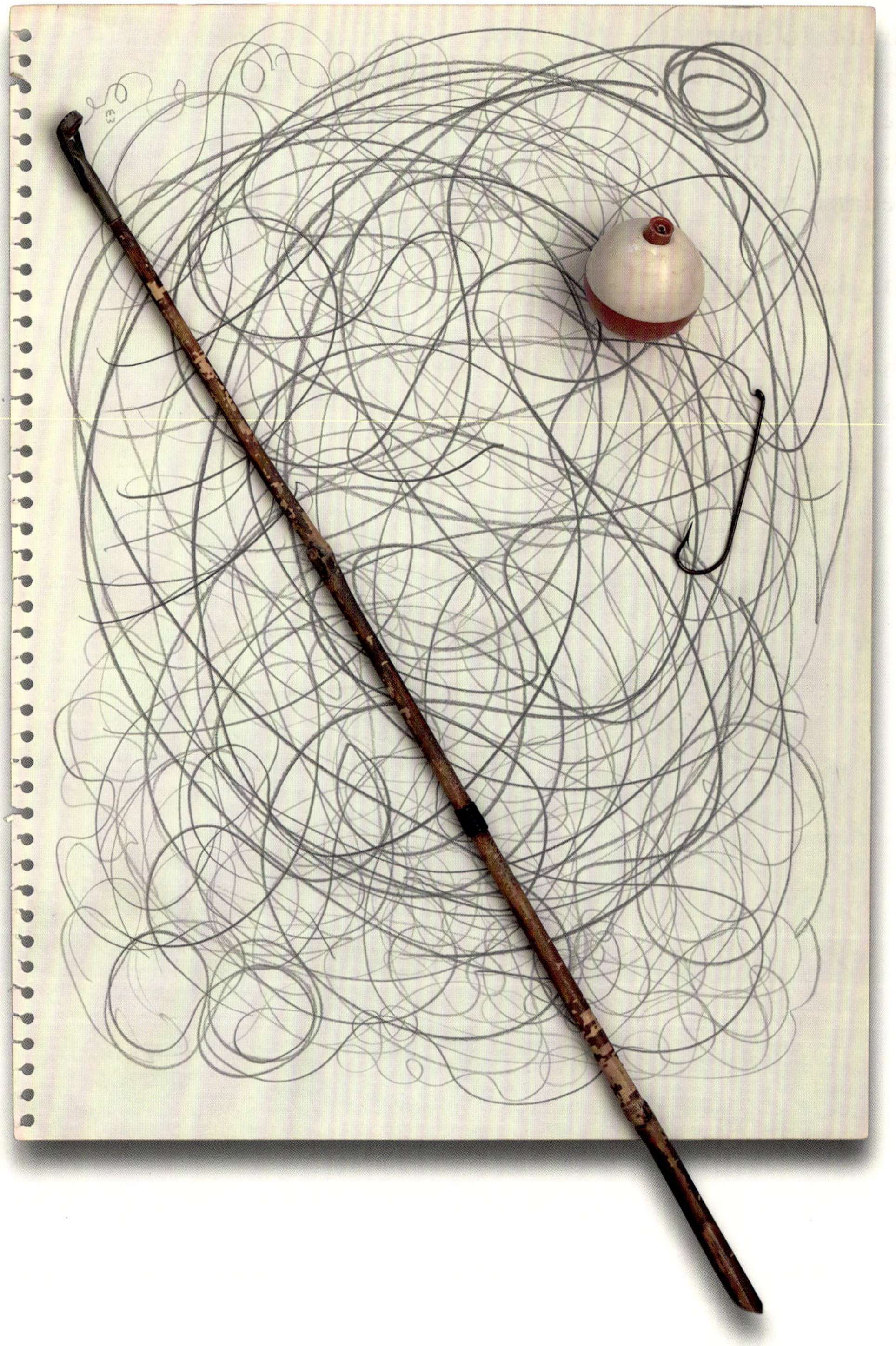

Image Credits

Thanks to the people of Cedar Rapids and the following institutions for photos of the Old Dam, the River, the Bridges and the Boatlocks:
Karl and Mary Koehler History Center
Masonic Temple
Cedar Rapids Public Works.

Thanks to the Waterloo Center for the Arts for the John Page Prints.

Photo on page 5 by John Whelan
Photos on title page and pages 6, 34, 47, 76, , 58, 59 and 76 by Jerry Grier
Photo on page 86 by National Park Staff, Effigy Mounds
Greeting card on pages 113 and 115, Hall Brothers Inc. (Hallmark) GE283-3
All other photos are from Schwarz family albums
Blueprints from Hedrick & Cochran Consulting Engineers
Print on page 14 by Japanese printmaker circa 1961
Drawing on page 23 by Jeremy Reinert
Prints on back cover and page137 by John Page circa 1969
Map of the neighborhood on page 55 by Roger Schwarz
Drawings on other pages by Dean Schwarz

Also by South Bear Press

Packin' Cats for the Arrr-Meee: Fun on the Farm in the 'Forties
By Geraldine Fromm Schwarz and John Fromm
Dean Schwarz, editor

In a rural childhood setting, another family member depicts the ways kids entertained themselves and learned life-lessons similar to those learned by the Boy in this companion piece to *The Boy and The Old Dam*.

www.southbearpress.org